Patricia Roberts

*v*ariations

Patricia *Roberts*

v a r i a t i o n s

KNITTING PATTERNS FOR MORE THAN 50 SEASONAL DESIGNS

GROVE WEIDENFELD
NEW YORK

Published by Grove Weidenfeld
A division of Grove Press, Inc.
841 Broadway
New York, NY 10003-4793

First published in Great Britain in 1991 by
Conran Octopus Limited, London.

**The designs in this publication may not be knitted for resale.
All rights reserved.**

Library of Congress Cataloging-in-Publication Data
Roberts, Patricia
    Variations: knitting patterns for more than fifty
seasonal designs /
Patricia Roberts – 1st American ed.
    p.   cm.
    ISBN 0-8021-1490-3
    1. Knitting-patterns.   2. Sweaters.   I. Title
    TT825.R633   1992
    746.9′2—dc 20   91-36901
                            CIP

Art Director   Mary Evans
Art Editor   Vanessa Courtier
Editor   Denise Bates
American Editor   Mary Flower
Editorial Assistant   Lynne Drew
Production   Jackie Kernaghan
Illustrations   Connie Jude
Photographic Styling   Caroline Baker
Photography   Sheila Rock, Sam Brown and Vittoria Amati

Typeset by Litho Link Limited, Welshpool, Wales
Printed in China.

First American edition 1992

10 9 8 7 6 5 4 3 2 1

contents

Introduction　　　8

S P R I N G

PAGE I 2

Peony	14
Abstract	20
Variations	*28*
Simple	30
Tahiti	36
Kashmir	42

S U M M E R

PAGE 4 8

Paisley	50
Parrots	56
Variations	*62*
Lilacs	64
Bobbles	70
Angel Fish	74
Variations	*82*

A U T U M N

PAGE 8 4

Cats	86
Bears	92
Variations	*98*
Camels	100
Variations	*110*
Alpine	112
Variations	*118*

W I N T E R

PAGE I 2 0

Patchwork Roses	122
Twist	132
Variations	*136*
Spaghetti	138
Raj	142
Tea Rose	152
Variations	*156*

Sources	159
Acknowledgments	160

i n t r o d u c t i o n

My aim in this book was to provide a number of patterns which, when knitted in different yarns and colors, or with design variations, would suit two or more seasons. It is an idea which arose from the display of garments in my London shop, where I tend to keep each season's yarns and colors in a separate area. Although I do new designs for each season, I may also continue favorite designs from one season to the next, changing the yarn and colors and sometimes making design modifications so that the sweaters, jackets, vests and so on are appropriate to the new season's weather and mood. Looking around the shop, it is quite astonishing how totally different two garments knitted to the same basic pattern, but using very different materials and color combinations can look. The patterns which follow are intended to exploit this huge potential for variety. There is none of the frustration often experienced with knitting patterns when you spot a design you really like but find that it can only be knitted in thin cottons, at a time when winter is approaching, or in chunky wool while outside the sun is blazing. And you could of course knit all the variations of one pattern and have a superb collection of very different-looking designs.

H o w   t o   u s e   t h e   b o o k

In the different variations of these patterns, it is often only the yarn and needle sizes which change. All this information is found at the head of the pattern, and Materials, Colors and Needle Sizes are listed under the title of each seasonal variation. All you have to do, therefore, is to decide on the particular variation you want to knit and look at the materials needed. Needle sizes are coded so that within the pattern instructions sizes A, B and C are referred to. The Tension information (see right) appears before the main pattern if one tension is common to all the variations. Otherwise, if the tension differs, the information appears at the beginning of the instructions for that particular variation. The same applies to Measurements.

Next come the master pattern instructions. These are only separated when there are two substantially different variations, such as a jacket and a sweater, in which case the two sets of instructions appear separately under Jacket Pattern or Sweater Pattern. (You will see that the term "sweater" is used throughout the book to refer specifically to pullover designs, rather than to jackets, cardigans or vests.) Where only small design changes are needed for a variation, these are included in the body of the master pattern and clearly marked. Instructions for larger sizes are given in parentheses; they relate to the ascending order of size given in the measurements at the beginning.

FAR LEFT RAJ, *RIGHT* CAMELS

The photographs are organized seasonally. Each master pattern is accompanied by photographs of the variation appropriate to that season. Within each seasonal section there are also Variations pages, where photographs of variations on other designs suitable for that season are featured. The instructions for these variations are included with the master knitting pattern, in whichever season it appears.

Tension

The **golden rule** for knitting garments successfully is to work at the correct tension – this is the most important part of making sure that a garment knits up to the size you want.

The tension for each design or variation is given within every pattern (see left). As every knitter's tension varies slightly, it is vitally important to check your tension before beginning work by knitting a tension square. If you cannot obtain the correct tension using the needle size recommended in the instructions, use larger or smaller needles accordingly. You will need to use smaller needles if your tension is too loose – too few stitches and rows to the measure – or larger ones if it is too tight – too many stitches and rows to the measure.

Please note that the needle sizes given in the pattern are recommended starting points only and that the needle size actually used should be that on which the stated tension is obtained. If a garment is knitted at the recommended tension, the measurements will then correspond to those given in the pattern.

Colors

Where different colors are used for variations within a pattern, the colors are coded a., b., c., etc. throughout the master pattern. Thus there is no change in the pattern, whatever colors or variation you choose. This also applies to the charts (see overleaf).

Abbreviations

At the beginning of each knitting pattern, you will find a list of abbreviations which are particular to that pattern. Always read through this list before beginning work. As there are different ways of working stitches, please do not assume that you know how to work an abbreviation without reading its explanation at the beginning of the pattern. General abbreviations common to all the patterns are listed overleaf.

LEFT BOBBLES

C h a r t s

Each chart uses the colors of the variation for the season in which the master pattern appears. When knitting other seasons' variations, simply substitute the color codes for that variation for those on the chart.

M a k i n g   u p   a n d   p r e s s i n g

For the best results, we recommend the invisible seaming method for making up the garments. Place the first finger of the hand you are not sewing with between the two pieces of knitting to be joined, holding them edge to edge, with the right side of the work facing you. Secure the seaming yarn at one edge, making sure that the needle is on the right side of the work. Taking the needle to the second edge, insert it under the thread that lies between the first and second stitches and draw the yarn through. Take the needle back to the first edge and insert it under the thread between the first and second stitches and draw the yarn through. Take the yarn back to the second edge, inserting the needle under the thread above the one worked previously and draw the yarn through. Return to the first edge and work in the same way. Continue like this until the seam is complete. Working seams in this way, it is not necessary to use pins, for the number of rows to be joined usually matches exactly.

Do not press the knitting unless it is recommended in the pattern. Many of the hand-knit designs in this book rely on their texture for effect and this can be ruined by harsh pressing.

C l e a n i n g

Hand Washing Most hand-knitting yarns may be washed by hand, using mild detergents. Never use harsh detergents or biological products. Make sure that the temperature of the water does not exceed that recommended on the yarn label. After washing and rinsing thoroughly, spin the garment for a few seconds, without heat, in a spin dryer or in the spin-only cycle of a washing machine. Alternatively, excess moisture may be removed by rolling the garment in a towel. To dry, lay the garment flat on a towel away from direct heat or sunlight. Harsh sunlight can fade hand-knitted garments and radiators can scorch them.

Dry Cleaning Certain hand-knitting yarns need to be dry cleaned. Always check the yarn label. If hand knits are to be dry cleaned, make sure you use a reputable cleaner.

G e n e r a l   A b b r e v i a t i o n s

k.	knit
p.	purl
st.	stitch
tog.	together
g.st.	garter stitch
k.2tog.b.	knit 2 together through back of stitches
dec.	decrease, by working 2 stitches together
inc.	increase, by working twice into same stitch
sl.	slip
r.s.	right side
w.s.	wrong side
y.r.n.	yarn round needle
s.s.	stockinette stitch – knit on right side, purl on wrong side
r.s.s.	reverse stockinette stitch – knit on wrong side, purl on right side
single rib	knit 1 and purl 1 alternately
double rib	knit 2 and purl 2 alternately
up 1	pick up the loop which lies between the needles, slip it onto the left-hand needle and knit into the *back* of it
m.	main color
a.,b.,c.,d.,e., f.,g.,h.,i.,j., k.,l.,n.	contrast colors

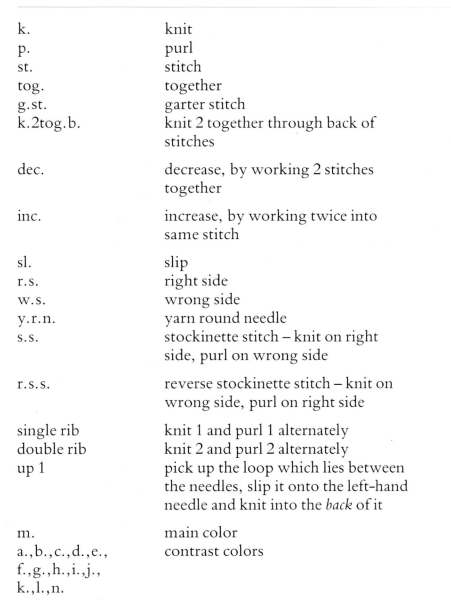

spring

After the chill winds of winter, spring sunshine brings color back to the earth; intense shades of green and the sudden burst of primary colors in flowers and foliage make one long to set aside the muted hues of the winter months. This spring collection contains designs to satisfy this longing for color. Peony and Tahiti pick up on the floral theme; Abstract and Kashmir have bold geometric and swirling motifs; while the Simple Sweater creates an exuberant splash of primary color. Versatile cotton comes into its own in spring, when balmy days may alternate with cooler weather, and it is used in various thicknesses in all of these designs.

FROM LEFT TO RIGHT:
PEONY SWEATER, ABSTRACT SWEATER, SIMPLE SWEATER, TAHITI SWEATER AND KASHMIR VEST

peony

A tie collar makes this child's cotton sweater look extra special. Alternative color combinations are given.

SPRING

Peony Sweater

PHOTOGRAPH THIS PAGE

Materials

6 (8) (9) 50 gram balls of "Patricia Roberts Cotton No.2" in main color and 1 50 gram ball of the same yarn in each of the 7 or 8 contrast colors, according to color combination chosen. A pair each of size 3 and size 5 Aero knitting needles.

Colors

m. = yellow, a. = red, b. = green, c. and e. = coral, d. = fuchsia, f. = orient blue, g. = mauve, h. = aqua.
or
m. = khaki, a. = red, b. = green, c. = coral, d. = fuchsia, e. = mauve, f. = orient blue, g. = yellow, h. = aqua.

Needle Sizes

Use size 5 needles for those referred to as size "A" and size 3 needles for those referred to as size "B" in the pattern.

Tension

12 stitches and 16 rows to 2 in (5 cm) over the pattern using size "A" needles.

Sweater Pattern

Measurements

	5-6 years (Size 1)	7-8 years (Size 2)	9-10 years (Size 3)
Underarms:	30 in (75 cm)	33 in (82.5 cm)	36 in (90 cm)
Side seam:	10 in (25 cm)	11 in (27.5 cm)	12¼ in (31 cm)
Length:	16 in (40 cm)	18 in (45 cm)	20 in (50 cm)
Sleeve seam:	11 in (27.5 cm)	13½ in (35 cm)	16 in (40 cm)

Peony Sweater
RIGHT

Back

With size "B" needles and m. cast on 93 (101) (109) sts.
and work 16 (20) (24) rows in single rib.
Change to size "A" needles and with m. work in
pattern as follows:

1st row: All k.
2nd row: K.1, ★ p.3, k.1; repeat from ★ to end.
3rd row: P.2, ★ k.1, p.3; repeat from ★ ending last
repeat p.2.
4th row: As 2nd row.
5th row: All k.
6th row: P.2, ★ k.1, p.3; repeat from ★ ending last
repeat p.2.
7th row: K.1, ★ p.3, k.1; repeat from ★ to end.
8th row: As 6th row.

The last 8 rows form the pattern. Repeat them 5 (7) (8)
times, then work the first 6 (2) (2) rows again.

For third size only:

Mark each end of the last row with colored threads to

denote armholes, then pattern 4 more rows.

For all sizes:

Now working in pattern as set in m. and working the
color patterns from the charts in s.s. continue as
follows: Use separate balls of m. at each side of the
color motifs and separate small balls of contrast colors
for each motif, so that colors not in use are not taken
across the back of the work.

1st row: With m. pattern 67 (75) (79), then from chart
A with b. k.3, with m. pattern 23 (23) (27).
2nd row: With m. pattern 23 (23) (27), from chart A
with b. p.4, with m. pattern 66 (74) (78).

On second size only:

Mark each end of the last row with colored threads to
denote armholes.

For all sizes:

3rd row: With m. pattern 64 (72) (76), from chart A
with b. k.4, with c. k.1, with b. k.1, with m. pattern
23 (23) (27).

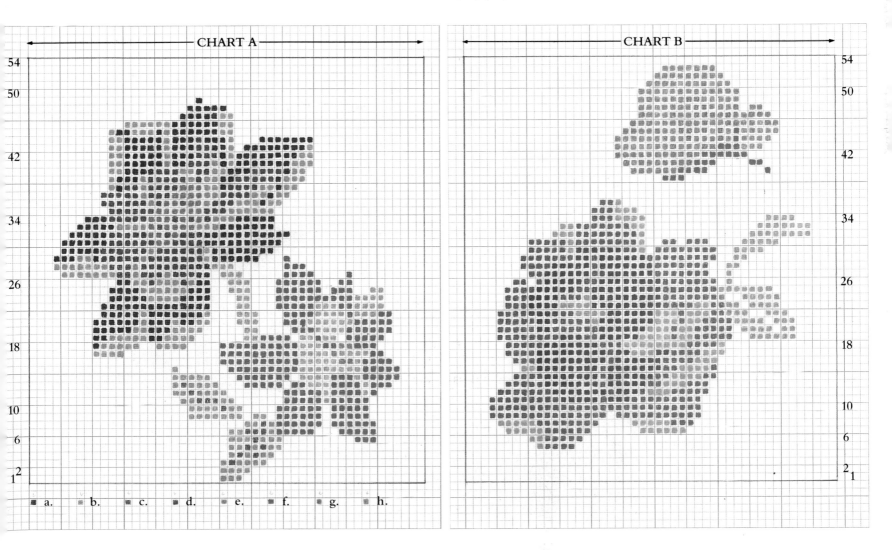

CHART A

CHART B

54 50 42 34 26 18 10 6 1 2

a. b. c. d. e. f. g. h.

4th row: With m. pattern 24 (24) (28), with b. p.1, with c. p.1 twice, with b. p.2, with m. pattern 63 (71) (75).

5th row: With m. pattern 32 (32) (36), then from chart B with d. k.4, with e. k.1, with m. pattern 25 (33) (33), from chart A with b. k.2, with c. k.1, with b. k.1, with c. k.1, with b. k.2, with m. pattern 24 (24) (28).

6th row: With m. pattern 24 (24) (28), from chart A with b. p.3, with c. p.1, with b. p.3, with m. p.9, with f p.3, then with m. pattern 12 (20) (20), then from chart B with e. p.2, with d. p.5, with m. pattern 31 (31) (35).

The last 6 rows set the position of the patterns given in charts A and B.

Work the 7th to 54th pattern rows from the charts as set, marking each end of the 10th pattern row with colored threads to denote armholes on the first size.

To slope the shoulders: Bind off 14 (15) (16) sts. at the beginning of the next 2 rows, then 13 (15) (17) sts. at the beginning of the 2 following rows.

Bind off the remaining 39 (41) (43) sts. loosely.

Front

Work as given for back until the 31st (29th) (27th) pattern row has been worked from the charts. Now divide the sts. for the neck:

Next row: Pattern 46 (50) (54) and leave these sts. on a spare needle until required for right front shoulder, bind off 1 st., pattern to end and continue on these 46 (50) (54) sts. for the left front shoulder.

Left front shoulder: To shape the neck: Dec. 1 st. at the neck edge on each of the next 19 (20) (21) rows. On 27 (30) (33) sts. work 3 (4) (5) rows. Work 1 extra row here, when working right front shoulder.

To slope the shoulder: Bind off 14 (15) (16) sts. at the beginning of the next row. On 13 (15) (17) sts. work 1 row, then bind off.

Right front shoulder: With right side of work facing rejoin yarn to inner edge of sts. left on spare needle and work as given for left front shoulder, noting the

variation in the rows, before sloping the shoulder.

Sleeves

Both alike: With size "B" needles and a. cast on 41 (49) (57) sts., break off a., join in m. and work 16 (20) (24) rows in single rib.

Change to size "A" needles and work in pattern as follows:

1st to 8th rows: With m. in main pattern as given for back.

9th and 10th rows: With e. all k.

The last 10 rows form the sleeve pattern, but the successive repeats of the 9th and 10th rows are worked in the color sequence of g., f., h., d., a. and then commence with e. again.

Thus continuing in pattern, work 6 rows straight, then inc. 1 st. at each end of the next row and then every 4th row 12 (14) (16) times.

On 67 (79) (91) sts. pattern 7 (15) (23) rows.
Bind off loosely.

Half Collar

2 pieces alike: With size "B" needles and m. cast on 29 (30) (31) sts. and work in moss st. as follows:

Moss st. row: K.1, ★ p.1, k.1; repeat from ★ to end.
Repeat this row 7 times more.

Continuing in moss st. as set, dec. 1 st. at the beginning of the next row and then every 8th row 25 (26) (27) times, then on the following 4th row.
[2 sts.]
Take the 2 remaining sts. tog. and fasten off.

Making Up

Do not press. Join shoulder seams. Sew bound off edges of sleeves to the straight row ends between the marking threads on back and front. Join sleeve and side seams. Join cast on edges of collar pieces. Neatly sew the straight row end edges of the collar in place, with the collar seam positioned at center back neck, and ending ½ in (1 cm) from center front neck. Leave the extra length on the collar free to tie.

a b s t r a c t

Dynamic circles, triangles and zigzags shoot across this design for a sweater and a cardigan.

SPRING

Abstract Cardigan
PHOTOGRAPH THIS PAGE

Materials
8 50 gram balls of "Patricia Roberts Cotton No.2" in main color and for the contrast colors, 2 balls of the same yarn in d. and 1 ball in e.; plus, in 50 gram balls of "Patricia Roberts Extra Thick Cotton," 2 balls in each of the contrasts b. and c. and 1 ball in each of the contrasts a. and f. A pair each of size 3 and size 2 Aero knitting needles, a medium-size cable needle and 3 buttons.

Colors
m. = white, a. = yellow, b. = red, c. = orient blue, d. = black, e. = sap green, f. = mauve.

Needle Sizes
Use size 3 needles for those referred to as size "A" and size 2 for those referred to as size "B".

SPRING

Abstract Sweater
PHOTOGRAPH THIS PAGE

Materials
10 (11) 50 gram balls of "Patricia Roberts Cotton No.2" in main color and for the contrast colors, 2 balls of the same yarn in each of the contrasts c. and d. and 1 ball in e.; plus, in 50 gram balls of "Patricia Roberts Extra Thick Cotton," 2 balls in each of the contrasts a., b. and f.
For the medium size: A pair each of size 3 and size 2 Aero knitting needles.
For the large size: A pair each of size 3 and size 5 Aero knitting needles.

Colors
m. = yellow, a. = red, b. = orient blue, c. = fuchsia, d. = black, e. = sap green, f. = mauve.

SPRING

Abstract Cardigan
CENTER RIGHT

Abstract Sweater
ABOVE RIGHT, BELOW RIGHT
AND OPPOSITE

AUTUMN

Abstract Cardigan
PAGE 118

Needle Sizes

For the medium size: Use size 3 needles for those referred to as size "A" and size 2 for those referred to as size "B" in the pattern.

For the large size: Use size 5 needles for those referred to as size "A" and size 3 for those referred to as size "B" in the pattern.

AUTUMN

Abstract Cardigan

PHOTOGRAPH PAGE 118

Materials

9 50 gram balls of "Patricia Roberts Pure Wool No.2" in main color and one 100 gram ball of "Patricia Roberts Extra Thick Wool" in each of the 6 contrast colors. A pair each of size 5 and size 3 Aero knitting needles, a medium-size cable needle and 3 buttons.

Colors

m. = black, a. = khaki, b. = faded violet, c. = airforce blue, d. = warm brown, e. = olive, f. = donkey brown.

Needle Sizes

Use size 5 needles for those referred to as size "A" and size 3 needles for those referred to as size "B" in the pattern.

Abbreviations

c.4f., cable 4 front thus, slip next 2 sts. onto cable needle at front of work, k.2, then k.2 from cable needle.

Cardigan Pattern

Tension

13 stitches and 17 rows to 2 in (5 cm) over the stockinette stitch using size "A" needles.

Measurements

Underarms: 44½ in (112.5 cm). Side seam: 10 in (25 cm). Length: 19¾ in (49 cm). Sleeve seam: 15 in (37.5 cm).

Back

With size "B" needles and m. cast on 128 sts. and work 7 rows in single rib.

Increase row: Rib 4, ★ up 1, rib 8; repeat from ★ ending last repeat rib 4. [144 sts.]

Change to size "A" needles and work in pattern from chart as follows. The pattern is worked entirely in s.s., so only the color details are given. Use separate small balls of color for each section of the pattern, so that colors not in use are not taken across the back of the work. ★★

1st row: 16 m., 4 e., 55 m., 3 f., 66 m.

2nd row: 55 m., 3 f., 8 m., 3 f., 52 m., 7 e., 16 m.

The last 2 rows set the position of the pattern, given in the chart. Work the 3rd to 76th rows from the chart.

To shape the armholes: Continuing in pattern from chart, work as follows:

1st Shaping row: Bind off 6 sts., work across next 11 sts. and slip these 12 sts. onto a safety pin until required, pattern to end.

2nd Shaping row: As 1st row. [108 sts.]

Continuing in pattern from chart, work 30 rows straight, then inc. 1 st. at each end of the next row and then every 4th row 7 times, then on the 6 following alternate rows.

On 136 sts, work 1 row.

160

154

146

138

130

122

114

106

98

90

82

74

66

58

50

42

34

26

18

10

1

a.   b.   c.   d.   e.   f.

To slope the shoulders: Bind off 8 sts. at the beginning of the next 6 rows and 12 sts. on the 4 following rows. Bind off the remaining 40 sts.

Left Front

With size "B" needles and m., cast on 64 sts. and, noting that there will be 72 sts. after the increase row, work as given for back until ** is reached.
1st row: 16 m., 4 e., 52 m.
2nd row: 49 m, 7 e., 16 m.
The last 2 rows set the position of the pattern on the right-hand side of the chart. Work the 3rd to 56th rows from the chart as set.
***To slope the front edge**: Continuing in pattern from chart, dec. 1 st. at the end of the next row and then every 4th row 4 times.
On 67 sts. pattern 3 rows.
To shape the armhole:
Shaping row: Bind off 6 sts., work across next 11 sts. and slip these 12 sts. onto a safety pin until required, pattern until 2 remain, dec. for front edge.
Pattern 3 rows.

Dec. 1 st. at the end – front edge – on the next row and then every 4th row 6 times.
On 41 sts. pattern 3 rows.
Inc. 1 st., for armhole, at the beginning and dec. 1 st. for front edge, at the end of the next row and then every 4th row 6 times.
On 41 sts. pattern 3 rows. Then, continuing to shape the armhole edge only, inc. 1 st. at the beginning of the next row and the 6 following alternate rows.
On 48 sts. work 1 row.
To slope the shoulder: Bind off 8 sts. at the beginning of the next row and the 2 following alternate rows, then 12 sts. on the following alternate row. On 12 sts. work 1 row, then bind off.

Right Front

With size "B" needles and m., cast on 64 sts. and, noting that there will be 72 sts. after the increase row, work as given for back until ** is reached.
1st row: 3 m., 3 f., 66 m.
2nd row: 55 m., 3 f., 8 m., 3 f., 3 m.
The last 2 rows set the position of the pattern on the left-hand side of the chart. Work the 3rd to 57th rows from the chart as set.
Continuing in pattern, from left-hand side of chart as set, work as given for left front from *** to end.

Armbands

4 alike: With right side of work facing, rejoin m. to the 12 sts. left on safety pin at armhole edge and using size "A" needles, work as follows:
1st row: K.2, sl.1, k.1, p.s.s.o., y.r.n., k.4, y.r.n., k.2tog., k.2.
2nd row: K.2, p.8, k.2.
3rd and 4th rows: As 1st and 2nd rows.
5th row: K.2, sl.1, k.1, p.s.s.o., y.r.n., c.4f. y.r.n., k.2tog., k.2.
6th row: As 2nd row.
7th and 8th rows: As 1st and 2nd rows.
The last 8 rows form the cable pattern; repeat them 8 times more, then bind off.

Sleeves

Both alike: With size "B" needles and m. cast on 60 sts. and work 12 rows in single rib.
**Change to size "A" needles and noting the information given for color work for back, work in pattern from chart as follows:
1st row: 33 m., 3 f., 24 m.
2nd row: 13 m., 3 f., 8 m., 3 f., 33 m.
The last 2 rows set the position of the pattern given at the center of the chart. Work the 3rd to 6th rows as set.

Continuing in pattern and working the extra sts. into the pattern as they occur, inc. 1 st. at each end of the next row and then every 6th row 17 times. On 96 sts. pattern 7 rows. ★★

To shape the sleeve top: Bind off 6 sts. at the beginning of the next 2 rows, then dec. 1 st. at each end of the next row and the 10 following alternate rows. Bind off the remaining 62 sts.

Frontband
With size "B" needles and m. cast on 8 sts. and work 6 rows in single rib.
1st Buttonhole row: Rib 3, bind off 2, rib to end.
2nd Buttonhole row: Rib 3, turn, cast on 2 over those bound off, turn, rib to end.
Rib 26 rows.
Repeat the last 28 rows once more, then work the 2 buttonhole rows again.
Continue in rib, until the band is long enough to fit up right front edge, with last buttonhole in line with first front edge decrease, across back neck edge and down left front edge. Do not bind off.

Making Up
Neatly sew row ends of armbands in position. Join shoulder seams. Set in sleeves. Join sleeve and side seams. Sew frontband in place, binding off when correct length is assured. Sew on buttons.

Sweater Pattern

Tension
For the medium size: 13 stitches and 17 rows to 2 in (5 cm) over stockinette stitch using size "A" needles and m.
For the large size: 12 stitches and 16 rows to 2 in (5 cm) over stockinette stitch using size "A" needles and m.

Measurements
For the medium size:
Underarms: 44 in (110 cm). Side seam: 18 in (45 cm). Length: 27 in (67 cm). Sleeve seam: 16 in (40 cm).
For the large size:
Underarms: 48 in (120 cm). Side seam: 19 in (47.5 cm). Length: 28½ in (71 cm). Sleeve seam: 17 in (42.5 cm).

Back
With size "B" needles and m. cast on 132 sts. and work 19 rows in double rib.
Increase row: Rib 5, ★ up 1, rib 11; repeat from ★

ending last repeat rib 6. [144 sts.]

Change to size "A" needles and work the first 2 rows from the chart as given for Cardigan Pattern.

The last 2 rows set the position of the pattern, given in the chart. Work the 3rd to 132nd rows from the chart.

Mark each end of the last row with colored threads to denote armholes.

Work the 133rd to 160th rows from the chart, then work the first 44 rows again.

To slope the shoulders: Bind off 24 sts. at the beginning of the next 4 rows.

Bind off the remaining 48 sts.

Front

Work as given for back until 160 rows have been worked in pattern from chart, then work the first 19 rows again.

Now divide the sts. for the neck:

Next row: Pattern 60 sts. and leave these sts. on a spare needle, until required for right front shoulder, bind off 24 sts. for neck, pattern to end and continue on these 60 sts. for the left front shoulder.

Left front shoulder: To shape the neck: Dec. 1 st. at the neck edge on each of the next 12 rows.

On 48 sts. pattern 12 rows.

To slope the shoulder: Bind off 24 sts. at the beginning of the next row. On 24 sts. work 1 row, then bind off.

Right front shoulder: With right side of work facing rejoin yarn to inner edge of sts. left on spare needle and work to end of row, then work as given for left front shoulder to end.

Neckband: First join right shoulder seam. With right side of work facing, rejoin m. and using size "B" needles pick up and k. 27 sts. from left front neck edge, 24 sts. from center front, 27 sts. from right front neck edge and 48 sts. from back neck edge.

On 126 sts. work 9 rows in double rib, then bind off in rib.

Sleeves

Both alike: With size "B" needles and m. cast on 48 sts. and work 19 rows in single rib.

Increase row: Rib 2, ★ up 1, rib 4; repeat from ★ ending last repeat rib 2. [60 sts.]

Work as given for sleeves of Cardigan Pattern from ★★ to ★★. Bind off.

Making Up

Join left shoulder seam. Set in sleeves. Join sleeve and side seams.

spring *variations*

Camels Sweater

LEFT
Camels and a desert town dominate
this sweater with its border pattern
of sand dunes. Knitted in fine cotton,
it uses appropriate shades of sand
and taupe.
PATTERN PAGE 100

Patchwork Roses Jacket

RIGHT
The cotton yarn used for this hooded
jacket allows the patchwork design to
be seen to full effect.
PATTERN PAGE 122

Tea Rose T-shirt

FAR RIGHT
Delicate tea rose motifs are scattered
over a bright mustard background
on this versatile T-shirt.
PATTERN PAGE 152

s i m p l e

This design really does live up to its name – it is superbly quick and easy to knit and extraordinarily versatile. Sizes are given for a one-year-old right up to an adult. The photographs show a selection of colors and sizes but there is no limit to the combinations which can be chosen – the woman's sweater, for example, could easily be knitted in a multicolor version, or the child's in any one of a huge range of colors.

SPRING

Multicolor Simple Sweater

PHOTOGRAPH THIS PAGE

Materials
2 (2) (3) (3) (4) (4) (6) (6) 50 gram balls of "Patricia Roberts Extra Thick Cotton" in main color and 1 (2) (2) (2) (3) (3) (5) (5) balls of the same yarn in each of the 3 contrast colors, a., b. and c. A pair each of size 5 and size 6 Aero knitting needles and 3 buttons.

Colors
m. = mauve, a. = aqua blue, b. = pink, c. = yellow.

Needle Sizes
Use size 6 needles for those referred to as size "A" and size 5 needles for those referred to as size "B" in the pattern.

SPRING

One-color Simple Sweater

PHOTOGRAPH THIS PAGE

Materials
4 (5) (6) (8) (9) (11) (17) (17) 100 gram balls of "Patricia Roberts Extra Thick Cotton." A pair each of size 5 and size 6 Aero knitting needles and 3 buttons.

Color
White, pink or red

SPRING

Multicolor Simple Sweater
RIGHT

One-color Simple Sweater
RIGHT AND OVERLEAF

AUTUMN

Multicolor Simple Sweater
PAGE 110

One-color Simple Sweater
PAGE 111

Needle Sizes
Use size 6 needles for those referred to as size "A" and size 5 needles for those referred to as size "B" in the pattern.

AUTUMN

Multicolor Simple Sweater

PHOTOGRAPH PAGE 110

Materials
1 (1) (1) (2) (2) (2) (3) (3) 100 gram balls of "Patricia Roberts Extra Thick Wool" in main color and 1 (1) (1) (1) (2) (2) (3) (3) balls of the same yarn in each of the 3 contrast colors, a., b. and c. A pair each of size 6 and size 7 Aero knitting needles and 3 buttons.

Colors
m. = faded violet, a = airforce blue, b. = donkey brown, c. = khaki.

Needle Sizes
Use size 7 needles for those referred to as size "A" and size 6 needles for those referred to as size "B" in the pattern.

AUTUMN

One-color Simple Sweater

PHOTOGRAPH PAGE 111

Materials
2 (3) (3) (4) (5) (6) (9) (9) 100 gram balls of "Patricia Roberts Extra Thick Wool." A pair each of size 6 and size 7 Aero knitting needles and 3 buttons.

Colors
Donkey brown or olive

Needle Sizes
Use size 7 needles for those referred to as size "A" and size 6 needles for those referred to as size "B" in the pattern.

S w e a t e r   P a t t e r n

Tension

10 stitches and 16 rows to 2 in (5 cm) over both the main pattern and the moss stitch.

Measurements

	1 year	2 years	4 years	6 years
Underarms:	22 in	25 in	28 in	31 in
	(55 cm)	(62.5 cm)	(70 cm)	(77 cm)
Side seam:	5½ in	7 in	8½ in	10 in
	(14 cm)	(17.5 cm)	(21 cm)	(25 cm)
Length:	10 in	12 in	14 in	16 in
	(25 cm)	(30 cm)	(35 cm)	(40 cm)
Sleeve seam:	6 in	8 in	10 in	12 in
	(15 cm)	(20 cm)	(25 cm)	(30 cm)

	8 years	10 years	medium	large
Underarms:	34 in	36 in	46 in	49 in
	(85 cm)	(90 cm)	(115 cm)	(122.5 cm)
Side seam:	11½ in	13 in	17½ in	16 in
	(29 cm)	(32.5 cm)	(44 cm)	(40 cm)
Length:	18 in	20 in	26 in	26 in
	(45 cm)	(50 cm)	(65 cm)	(65 cm)
Sleeve seam:	14 in	16 in	17 in	17 in
	(35 cm)	(40 cm)	(42.5 cm)	(42.5 cm)

Note

Instructions are for the multicolor version; for the one-color version disregard the color details.

Back

With size "B" needles and a. cast on 56 (64) (72) (78) (86) (92) (116) (124) sts. and work 10 (14) (18) (18) (22) (22) (26) (26) rows in single rib.
Change to size "A" needles, break off a., join in m. and work in main pattern as follows:
1st, 2nd and 3rd rows: All k.
4th row: All p.
These 4 rows form the pattern, repeat them 7 (9) (11) (14) (16) (19) (27) (24) times, then work the first 2 rows again. Mark each end of the last row with colored threads to denote armholes.
Break off m., join in b., and k. 1 row. ★★
1st moss st. row: ★ K.1, p.1; repeat from ★ to end.
2nd moss st. row: ★ P.1, k. 1; repeat from ★ to end.
Repeat these 2 rows 15 (17) (19) (21) (23) (25) (31) (37) times more, then work the 1st row again.
To slope the shoulders: Bind off 13 (17) (20) (23) (26) (29) (39) (42) sts. at the beginning of the next 2 rows.
Leave the remaining 30 (30) (32) (32) (34) (34) (38) (40) sts. on a spare needle until required.

Front

Work as given for back until ★★ is reached.
Working in moss st. as for back continue as follows: Now divide the sts. for the neck opening:
Next row: Moss st. 26 (30) (33) (36) (40) (43) (54) (58) and leave these sts. on a spare needle until required for right front shoulder, bind off 4 (4) (6) (6) (6) (6) (8) (8) sts., moss st. to end and continue on these 26 (30) (33) (36) (40) (43) (54) (58) sts. for the left front shoulder.
Left front shoulder: Moss st. 21 (23) (25) (27) (29) (31) (37) (47) rows.
To shape the neck: Bind off 2 sts. at the beginning of the next row, then dec. 1 st. at the neck edge on each of the next 11 (11) (11) (11) (12) (12) (13) (14) rows. On 13 (17) (20) (23) (26) (29) (39) (42) sts. moss st. 1 (3) (5) (7) (8) (10) (15) (16) rows.
To slope the shoulder: Bind off.
Right front shoulder: With right side of work facing rejoin b. to inner edge of sts. left on spare needle and work to end of row, then work as given for left front shoulder to end.
Neckband: First join shoulder seams. With right side of work facing join in c. to right front neck edge and using size "B" needles, pick up and k. 14 (16) (18) (20) (22) (24) (30) (34) sts. from left front neck edge, k. across the sts. on spare needle at back neck edge, then

pick up and k. 14 (16) (18) (20) (22) (24) (30) (34) sts. from right front neck edge.

On 58 (62) (68) (72) (78) (82) (98) (108) sts. work 5 (5) (7) (7) (7) (7) (9) (9) rows in single rib, then bind off in rib loosely, using a size "A" needle.

Buttonband: With right side of work facing rejoin c. to either left or right (according to sex) front neck opening and, using size "B" needles, pick up and k. 28 (30) (34) (36) (39) (41) (48) (58) sts. from the row end edges, including those of neckband.

Work 5 (5) (7) (7) (7) (7) (9) (9) rows in single rib, then bind off loosely with a size "A" needle.

Buttonhole band: Work as given for buttonband, until 1 (1) (3) (3) (3) (3) (3) (3) rows have been worked in single rib.

1st Buttonhole row: Rib 2 (2) (3) (3) (3) (3) (4) (4), ★ bind off 2 (2) (2) (2) (3) (3) (4) (4) ★★, rib next 8 (9) (10) (11) (11) (12) (13) (18) ★; repeat from ★ to ★, then from ★ to ★★, rib to end.

2nd Buttonhole row: Rib 2 (2) (3) (3) (3) (3)(4) (4), ★ turn, cast on 2 (2) (3) (3) (3) (3) (5) (5) sts. over those bound off, turn ★★, rib 9 (10) (10) (11) (12) (13) (15) (20) ★, repeat from ★ to ★, then repeat from ★ to ★★, rib to end. Rib 2 (2) (2) (2) (2) (2) (4) (4) rows, then bind off in rib loosely using a size "A" needle.

Left Sleeve

With size "B" needles and c. cast on 28 (31) (34) (37) (40) (43) (46) (49) sts. and work 10 (14) (18) (18) (22) (22) (26) (26) rows in single rib.

Change to size "A" needles, break off c. and join in a., then work 4 rows in main pattern as given for back. Continuing in main pattern, inc. 1 st. at each end of the next row and then every 4th (4th) (6th) (6th) (6th) (6th) (6th) (4th) row 6 (7) (8) (9) (10) (11) (16) (19) times.

On 42 (47) (52) (57) (62) (67) (80) (89) sts. pattern 9 (17) (9) (19) (25) (35) (9) (29) rows.

Bind off loosely.

Right Sleeve

Work as given for left sleeve, but using b. instead of c. and c. instead of a.

Making Up

Press lightly on the wrong side with a warm iron over a damp cloth. Sew bound off edges of sleeves to row ends between the marking threads on back and front. Join sleeve and side seams. Neatly sew row ends of button- and buttonhole bands to the group of sts. bound off at center front. Sew on buttons.

t a h i t i

The rich colors and motifs of Gauguin's Tahiti paintings were the inspiration for this design with its exotic South-Sea Island theme. The cotton sweater can be knitted in a longer version, with full-length sleeves, or in a short-sleeved cropped variation.

S P R I N G

L o n g   T a h i t i   S w e a t e r

PHOTOGRAPH THIS PAGE

Materials
11 50 gram balls of "Patricia Roberts Cotton No. 2" in main color, 2 balls in contrast a. and 1 ball in each of the 8 other contrast colors. A pair each of size 3 and size 5 Aero knitting needles and a medium-size cable needle.

Colors
m. = mauve, a. = white, b. = blue, c. = fuchsia, d. = coral, e. = black, f. = yellow, g. = red, h. = olive, j. = pink.

Needle Sizes
Use size 5 needles for those referred to as size "A" and size 3 needles for those referred to as size "B" in the pattern.

S P R I N G

S h o r t   T a h i t i   S w e a t e r

PHOTOGRAPH THIS PAGE

Materials
6 50 gram balls of "Patricia Roberts Cotton No. 2" in main color, and 1 ball in each of the 8 other contrast colors. A pair each of size 3 and size 5 Aero knitting needles and a medium-size cable needle.

Colors
m. and a. = white, b. = blue, c. = fuchsia, d. = coral, e. = black, f. = yellow, g. = red, h. = olive, j. = pink.

Needle Sizes
Use size 5 needles for those referred to as size "A" and

SPRING

Long Tahiti Sweater
ABOVE RIGHT,
BELOW RIGHT
AND OPPOSITE

Short Tahiti Sweater
CENTER RIGHT

172
168
160
152
144
136
128
120
112
104
96
88
80
72
64
56
48
40
32
24
16
8
1

size 3 needles for those referred to as size "B" in the pattern.

Abbreviations

c.8f., cable 8 front thus, slip next 4 sts. onto cable needle and leave at front of work, k.4, then k.4 from cable needle ■ **c.8b.**, cable 8 back thus, as c.8f., but leaving sts. on cable needle at back of work ■ **3 from 1**, thus, k.1, y.r.n., k.1 all into 1 st.

Tension

12 stitches and 16 rows to 2 in (5 cm) over stockinette stitch using size "A" needles.

Long Sweater Pattern

Measurements

Underarms: 47 in (118 cm). Side seam: 18½ in (46 cm). Length: 27½ in (69 cm). Sleeve seam: 17 in (42.5 cm).

Back

With size "B" needles and m. cast on 144 sts. and work 24 rows in double rib.

Change to size "A" needles and beginning with a k. row, s.s. 12 rows.

Now work in pattern from chart as follows. Where the pattern is worked in s.s., only the color details are given. Use separate, small balls of color for each section of the mofits, so that colors not in use are not taken across the back of the work.

1st row: 90 m., 1 a., 53 m.

2nd row: 53 m., 1 a., 90 m.

3rd row: 90 m., 2 a., 52 m.

4th row: 52 m., 3 a., 89 m.

5th row: 7 m., 2 g., 30 m., 2 h., 30 m., 2 f., 16 m., 3 a., 11 m., 2 b., 30 m., 2 c., 7 m.

The last 5 rows set the position of the pattern given in the chart.

Now work the 6th to 112th rows from the chart, marking each end of the last row with colored threads to denote armholes.

Work the 113th to 172nd rows from the chart. With m. s.s. 8 rows.

To slope the shoulders: Bind off 24 sts. at the beginning of the next 4 rows. [48 sts.]

Neckband: Change to size "B" needles and work 8 rows in double rib.

Bind off in rib the remaining 48 sts.

Front

Work as given for back until the armholes have been

marked.

★★ Work the 113th to 153rd pattern rows.

Now divide the sts. for the neck: Pattern 64 sts. and leave these sts. on a spare needle until required for right front shoulder, bind off 16, pattern to end and continue on these 64 sts. for the left front shoulder.

Left front shoulder: To shape the neck: Continuing in pattern from chart, dec. 1 st. at the neck edge on each of the next 16 rows.

On 48 sts. pattern 10 rows.

To slope the shoulder: Bind off 24 sts. at the beginning of the next row. On 24 sts. work 1 row, then bind off.

Right front shoulder: With right side of work facing, rejoin yarn to the inner edge of the sts. left on spare needle and work to end of row, then work as given for left front shoulder to end.

Neckband: With right side of work facing, rejoin m.

to left front shoulder and using size "B" needles, pick up and k. 28 sts. from left front neck edge, 16 sts. from center front, 28 sts. from right front neck edge. On 72 sts. work 7 rows in double rib, then bind off in rib. ★★

Sleeves

Both alike: With size "B" needles and m. cast on 54 sts. and work 23 rows in double rib.

Increase row: Rib 2, ★ up 1, rib 2; repeat from ★ to end. [80 sts.]

Change to size "A" needles and beginning with a k. row s.s. 12 rows.

Now noting the information regarding color work given for the back, work in pattern as follows:

1st row: 26 m., 1 a., 53 m.

2nd row: 53 m., 1 a., 26 m.

3rd row: 26 m., 2 a., 52 m.

4th row: 52 m., 3 a., 25 m.

5th row: 7 m., 2 f., 16 m., 3 a., 11 m., 2 b., 30 m., 2 c., 7 m.

6th row: 6 m., 4 c., 28 m., 4 b., 9 m., 2 a., 1 j., 1 a., 15 m., 4 f., 6 m.

The last 6 rows set the position of the pattern given on the left-hand side of the chart.

Continuing in pattern from chart and working the extra sts. in m. as they occur, inc. 1 st. at each end of the next row and then every 8th row 7 times.

On 96 sts. pattern 17 more rows. This completes the pattern from the chart.

Continuing with m. only in s.s., work 20 rows straight, then bind off.

Making Up

Pin out and press lightly on the wrong side with a cool iron over a dry cloth. Join shoulder seams. Set in sleeves, between the marking threads on back and front. Join sleeve and side seams. Press seams.

Short Sweater Pattern

Measurements

Underarms: 47 in (118 cm). Side seam: 6½ in (16 cm). Length: 15½ in (39 cm). Sleeve seam: 6 in (15 cm).

Back and Front

Both alike: With size "B" needles and m. cast on 144 sts. and work 12 rows in double rib.

Change to size "A" needles and, beginning with a k. row, s.s. 4 rows.

Noting the information regarding color work given for the back of the long sweater, work from chart as

follows, beginning at the 77th row.

77th row: With m. k.68, c.8f., k.68.

78th to 80th rows: All m. in s.s.

81st row: 47 m., 1 a. (note that m. and a. are the same for the white colorway), 70 m., 6 g., 4 d., 16 m.

82nd row: 16 m., 4 d., 8 g., 68 m., 1 a., 47 m.

The last 6 rows set the position of the pattern given in the chart. Now work the 83rd to 112th rows from the chart, marking each end of the last row with colored threads to denote armholes.

Work as given for front of Long Sweater Pattern from ★★ to ★★, including neckband

Sleeves

Both alike: With size "B" needles and m. cast on 80 sts. and work 4 rows in double rib.

Change to size "A" needles and beginning with a k. row, s.s. 4 rows. Now work in pattern as follows (where this is worked in s.s. only the color details are given):

1st row: 7 m., 2 b., 30 m., 2 c., 30 m., 2 d., 7 m.

2nd row: 6 m., 4 d., 28 m., 4 c., 28 m., 4 b., 6 m.

3rd row: 6 m., 4 b., 28 m., 4 c., 28 m., 4 d., 6 m.

4th row: 7 m., 2 d., 30 m., 2 c., 30 m., 2 b., 7 m.

5th to 11th rows: All m.

12th row: 34 m., then with m. k.2, p.8, k.2, then 34 m.

13th to 16th rows: Repeat 11th and 12th rows twice.

17th row: 36 m., with m. c.8f., 36 m.

18th row: As 12th row.

19th and 20th rows: As 11th and 12th rows.

21st row: 23 m., 2 f., 30 m., 2 g., 23 m.

22nd row: 22 m., 4 g., 8 m., with m. k.2, p.8, k.2, then in s.s. 8 m., 4 f., 22 m.

23rd row: With m. inc., then in s.s. 21 m., 4 f., 28 m., 4 g., 21 m., with m. inc.

24th row: 24 m., 2 g., 9 m., with m. k.2, p.8, k.2, then in s.s. 9 m., 2 f., 24 m.

25th row: With m. s.s. to center 8 sts., c.8f., s.s. to end.

26th row: With m. s.s. to center 12 sts., k.2, p.8, k.2. s.s. to end.

27th row: With m. in s.s.

28th row: As 26th row.

29th to 32nd row: Repeat 27th and 28th rows twice, increasing 1 st. at each end of the first of these rows.

33rd to 36th row: As 25th to 28th rows, increasing 1 st. at each end of the first of these rows.

37th to 40th rows: With m. in s.s., increasing 1 st. at each end of the first of these rows. [88 sts.]

Bind off loosely.

Making Up

As given for Long Sweater Pattern.

kashmir

The spring variation of this distinctive vest has a very striking feature – the back is composed entirely of blue and white stripes. The summer version, on the other hand, incorporates golden lurex into the pattern, bringing a luxurious sparkle to the design. The winter alternative is different again, with creamy cashmere or wool setting an elegant tone.

SPRING

Kashmir Vest

PHOTOGRAPH THIS PAGE

Materials
8 50 gram balls of "Patricia Roberts Cotton No.2" in main color and 4 balls of the same yarn in contrast a. A pair each of size 2 and size 3 Aero knitting needles, a fine cable needle and 4 buttons.

Colors
m. = white, a. = navy.

Needle Sizes
Use size 2 needles for those referred to as size "B" and size 3 needles for those referred to as size "A" in the pattern.

SUMMER

Kashmir Vest

PHOTOGRAPH PAGE 62

Materials
10 25 gram balls of "Patricia Roberts Fine Cotton" in main color and 3 25 gram balls of "Patricia Roberts Lurex" in contrast a. A pair each of size 1 and size 2 Aero knitting needles, a fine cable needle and 5 buttons.

Colors
m. = sand, a. = gold.

Needle Sizes
Use size 1 needles for those referred to as size "B" and size 2 needles for those referred to as size "A" in the pattern.

SPRING

Kashmir Vest
RIGHT

SUMMER

Kashmir Vest
PAGE 62

WINTER

Kashmir Vest
PAGE 156

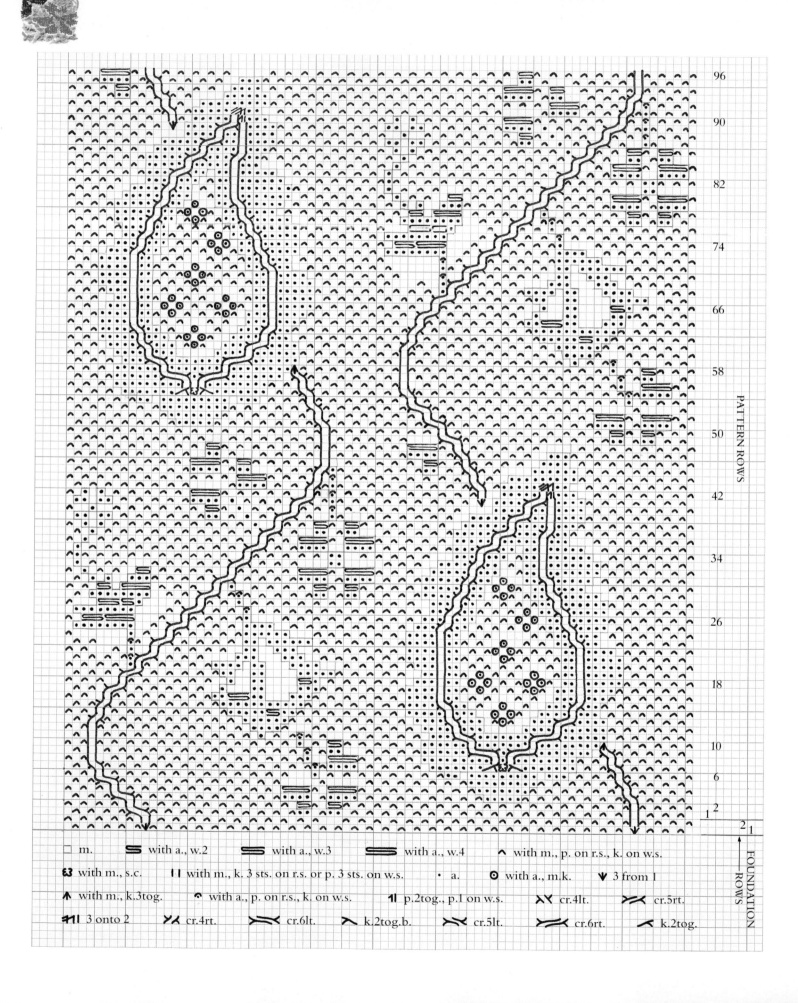

☐ m.　　　🝛 with a., w.2　　　🝛 with a., w.3　　　🝛 with a., w.4　　　⌢ with m., p. on r.s., k. on w.s.

🝛 with m., s.c.　　　❙❙ with m., k. 3 sts. on r.s. or p. 3 sts. on w.s.　　　• a.　　　⊙ with a., m.k.　　　↯ 3 from 1

⋏ with m., k.3tog.　　　⌣ with a., p. on r.s., k. on w.s.　　　🝛 p.2tog., p.1 on w.s.　　　✕✕ cr.4lt.　　　✕ cr.5rt.

🝛 3 onto 2　　　✕✕ cr.4rt.　　　✕ cr.6lt.　　　✕ k.2tog.b.　　　✕ cr.5lt.　　　✕ cr.6rt.　　　✕ k.2tog.

WINTER

Kashmir Vest

PHOTOGRAPH PAGE 156

Materials
12 25 gram balls of either "Patricia Roberts Pure Wool No.1" or "Patricia Roberts Cashmere." A pair each of size 2 and size 3 Aero knitting needles, a fine cable needle and 5 buttons.

Color
Cream

Needle Sizes
Use size 2 needles for those referred to as size "B" and size 3 needles for those referred to as size "A" in the pattern.

Abbreviations

3 from 1, k.1, y.r.n., k.1 all into 1 st. ■ **w.2**, wrap 2 thus, with a. p.2, ★ pass a. to back of work, sl. sts. just worked onto left-hand needle, bring a. to front of work, with a. p. these 2 sts. ★, repeat from ★ to ★ ■ **w.3 and w.4**, as w.2, but working over 3 or 4 sts.

instead of 2 as appropriate ■ **cr.4lt**, cross 4 left thus, sl. next 3 sts. onto cable needle at front of work, k.1, then k.3 from cable needle ■ **cr.4rt**, cross 4 right thus, sl. next st. onto cable needle at back of work, k.3, then k.1 from cable needle ■ **cr.5lt**, cross 5 left thus, sl. next 3 sts. onto cable needle at front of work, k.2, then k.3 from cable needle ■ **cr.5rt**, cross 5 right thus, sl. next 2 sts. onto cable needle at back of work, k.3, then k.2 from cable needle ■ **cr.6lt**, cross 6 left thus, sl. next 3 sts. onto cable needle at front of work, k.3, then k.3 from cable needle ■ **cr.6rt**, cross 6 right as cr.6lt., but leaving sts. on cable needle at back of work ■ **m.k.**, make knot thus, k. and p. into one st., turn, k.2, turn, k.2tog. ■ **3 onto 2**, thus, sl. 3rd, 4th and 5th sts. on left-hand needle over first 2 sts., with a. k. these 2 sts. ■ **s.c.**, start circle thus, k.1, y.r.n., k.1, y.r.n., k.1, all into one st., turn, p.5, turn, k.2, 3 from 1, k.2.

Spring Vest
Pattern

Tension
13 stitches and 19 rows to 2 in (5 cm) over the moss stitch using size "A" needles.

Measurements
Underarms: 47½ in (119 cm).
Side seam: 12½ in (31 cm).
Length: 22¾ in (57 cm).

Back
With size "B" needles and m. cast on 145 sts. and work in moss st. as follows:
Moss st. row: With m. k.1, ★ p.1, k.1; repeat from ★ to end.
Repeat this row 9 times.
Change to size "A" needles and then work in stripe pattern.
1st to 8th rows: With a. in s.s.
9th row: With m. all k.
10th to 18th rows: With m. in moss st.
The last 18 rows form the pattern; repeat them 5 times more.
To shape the armholes: Continuing in stripe pattern bind off 6 sts. at the beginning of the next 2 rows, then dec. 1 st. at each end of the next row and the 5 following alternate rows.
On 121 sts. pattern 79 rows.
To slope the shoulders: Bind off 11 sts. at the beginning of the next 4 rows and 12 sts. on the 2 following rows.

Bind off the remaining 53 sts.

Armbands (Both alike): With right side of work facing, rejoin m. and using size "B" needles pick up and k. 68 sts. from armhole edge.

Work 5 rows in moss st., then bind off loosely.

Left Front

First work the pocket back as follows:

With size "B" needles and m. cast on 33 sts. and work 32 rows in moss st., then leave on a spare needle until required.

With size "B" needles and m. cast on 81 sts. and work 10 rows in moss st. as for back.

Change to size "A" needles and work in pattern as follows:

1st Foundation row: With m. k.1, (p.1, k.1) 3 times, 3 from 1, (k.1, p.1) 31 times, 3 from 1, (p.1, k.1) 5 times.

2nd Foundation row: (K.1, p.1) 5 times, p. the 3 sts. made from 1 st. on last row, (p.1, k.1) 31 times, p.3, k.1, (p.1, k.1) 3 times.

Now work in the repeat pattern from the chart as follows:

1st row: With m. k.1, (p.1, k.1) 3 times, k. the 3 sts. represented by 1 square of the chart, (k.1, p.1) 18 times, k.1, with a. k.2, with m. p.1, k.1, with a. k.2, with m. p.1, (k.1, p.1) 9 times, cr.5lt, (p.1, k.1) 4 times.

2nd row: With m. (k.1, p.1) 4 times, p. the 3 sts. shown in 1 square, (p.1, k.1) 10 times, p.1, with a. w.2, with m. k.1, p.1, with a. w.2, with m. k.1, (p.1, k.1) 18 times, p.3, k.1, (p.1, k.1) 3 times.

The last 4 rows set the position of the pattern.

Work the 3rd to 32nd rows from the chart.

Pocket row: Pattern 32, slip next 33 sts. onto a stitch holder until required for pocket top and, in their place, work across the 33 sts. of pocket back and pattern to end.

Work the 34th to 94th rows from the chart.

To slope the front edge: Maintaining the continuity of the 96-row repeat pattern as set, dec. 1 st. at the end of the next row and the 5 following alternate rows. On 75 sts. work 1 row.

To shape the armhole and continue to slope the front edge: Bind off 6 sts. at the beginning and dec. 1 st. at the end of the next row, then dec. 1 st. at each end of the 6 following alternate rows. [56 sts.]

Dec. 1 st. at the end – front edge – on the 22 following alternate rows.

On 34 sts. pattern 35 rows.

To slope the shoulder: Bind off 11 sts. at the beginning of the next row and the following alternate

row. On 12 sts. work 1 row, then bind off.

Pocket top: With right side of work facing, rejoin m. to the 33 sts. on stitch holder and using size "B" needles work 6 rows in moss st., then bind off.

Armband: As given for back.

Right Front

Work as given for left front, omitting pocket back, until the 32nd pattern row has been worked.

Work the 33rd to 95th rows from the chart.

To slope the front edge: Work as given for left front edge shaping to end.

Armband: As given for back.

Frontband: First join shoulder seams. With size "B" needles and m. cast on 7 sts. and work 6 rows in moss st.

1st Buttonhole row: Moss st. 2, bind off 3, moss st. to end.

2nd Buttonhole row: Moss st. 2, turn, cast on 3 over those bound off, turn, moss st. 2.

Moss st. 30 rows.

Repeat the last 32 rows twice more, then work the 2 buttonhole rows again.

Continue in moss st. until the band is long enough to fit up right front edge (so that the last buttonhole row is in line with first front edge dec.), across back neck

edge and down left front edge. Sew in place, binding off when correct length is assured.

Making Up
Do not press. Join side seams. Catch pocket back in place on wrong side, neatly sew row ends of pocket top in position. Sew on buttons.

Summer & Winter Vest Patterns

Tension
16 stitches and 22 rows to 2 in (5 cm) over the moss st. using size "A" needles.

Measurements
Underarms: 38½ in (96 cm). Side seam: 10¾ in (27 cm). Length: 19½ in (49 cm).

For the Summer Vest:
Work as given for the Spring Vest Pattern.

For the Winter Vest:
Work as given for the Spring Vest Pattern, but use m. for both m. and a.

Summer

This is the season to go to town on dazzling shades and dramatic designs. No color can be too bright for the sunny days and sultry evenings of summer and this collection covers a range from mustard yellow to startling aqua blue. If the weather is hot, sweaters and jackets need to be cool, and cotton makes them light enough to wear in the heat of the day, yet warm enough to reach for in the cooler hours when the sun has gone down. From the rich patterning of Parrots, Lilacs and Angel Fish to the simpler, one-color designs of Paisley and Bobbles, there is something here for every taste and every level of expertise.

FROM LEFT TO RIGHT:
PAISLEY SWEATER, PARROTS CARDIGAN, LILACS SWEATER,
BOBBLES JACKET AND ANGEL FISH CARDIGAN

p a i s l e y

The curving shapes of traditional paisley patterns were the inspiration for this one-color design. Knitted in cotton or wool, it has long and short versions of the sweater. The long sweater also includes a larger size for a man.

S U M M E R

Long Paisley Sweater

PHOTOGRAPH THIS PAGE

Materials
17 50 gram balls of "Patricia Roberts Cotton No.2" (plus 1 extra ball for the man's size). A pair each of size 5 and size 3 Aero knitting needles and a medium-size cable needle.

Color
Mustard

Needle Sizes
Use size 5 needles for those referred to as size "A" in the pattern and size 3 needles for those referred to as size "B" in the pattern.

A U T U M N

Short Paisley Sweater

PHOTOGRAPH PAGE 99

Materials
12 50 gram balls of "Patricia Roberts Pure Wool No. 2." A pair each of size 5 and size 3 Aero knitting needles and a medium-size cable needle.

Color
Olive

Needle Sizes
Use size 5 needles for those referred to as size "A" in the pattern and size 3 needles for those referred to as size "B" in the pattern.

S U M M E R

Long Paisley Sweater
RIGHT

A U T U M N

Short Paisley Sweater
PAGE 99

W I N T E R

Long Paisley Sweater
PAGE 156

WINTER

Long Paisley Sweater

PHOTOGRAPH PAGE 156

Materials
16 50 gram balls of "Patricia Roberts Pure Wool No. 2" (plus 1 extra ball for the man's size). A pair each of size 5 and size 6 Aero knitting needles and a medium-size cable needle.

Color
Cream

Needle Sizes
Use size 6 needles for those referred to as size "A" in the pattern and size 5 needles for those referred to as size "B" in the pattern.

Abbreviations
3 from 1, thus, k.1, y.r.n., k.1 all into one st. ■ **c.4b.**, cable 4 back thus, slip next 2 sts. onto cable needle at back of work, k.2, then k.2 from cable needle ■ **c.4f.**, cable 4 front thus, slip next 2 sts. onto cable needle at front of work, k.2, then k.2 from cable needle ■ **c.8f.**, cable 8 front thus, slip next 4 sts. onto cable needle at front of work, k.4, then k.4 from cable needle ■ **c.8b.**, cable 8 back, as c.8f., but leaving sts. on cable needle at back of work ■ **m.k.**, make knot thus, k.1, y.r.n.,

k.1 all into one st., turn, p.3, turn, pick up the loop originally worked into and slip it onto left-hand needle, then pass the 3 sts., just worked, over it, then k. this st. ■ **cr.4lt.**, cross 4 left thus, slip next 3 sts. onto cable needle at front of work, k.1, then k.3 from cable needle ■ **cr.4rt.**, cross 4 right thus, slip next st. onto cable needle at back of work, k.3, then k.1 from cable needle ■ **cr.5lt.**, cross 5 left thus, slip next 3 sts. onto cable needle at front of work, k.2, then k.3 from cable needle ■ **cr.5rt.**, cross 5 right thus, slip next 2 sts. onto cable needle at back of work, k.3, then k.2 from cable needle ■ **cr.6lt.**, cross 6 left thus, slip next 3 sts. onto cable needle at front of work, k.3, then k.3 from cable needle ■ **cr.6rt.**, cross 6 right thus, slip next 3 sts. onto cable needle and leave at back of work, k.3, then k.3 from cable needle ■ **s.p.**, start paisley thus, k.1, y.r.n., k.1, y.r.n., k.1 all into one st., turn, p.5, turn, k.2, up 1, k.1, up 1, k.2.

Special Note
When counting stitches, count the groups of 3 stitches represented by one square of the chart as one stitch. When decreasing across these groups of stitches, work 4 stitches together instead of 2.

Long Sweater Pattern

Tension
11 stitches and 16 rows to 2 in (5 cm) over the moss stitch, using size "A" needles. Worked at this tension

over the moss stitch, the 155 stitches across the back will measure 23 in (57.5 cm) in width and 96 rows – 1 repeat – of the pattern will measure 12 in (30 cm) in depth.

Measurements
Underarms: 46 in (115 cm). Side seam: 20 in (50 cm). Length: 28 in (70 cm). Sleeve seam: woman's 17 in (42.5 cm); man's 19 in (47.5 cm).

Back
With size "B" needles cast on 140 sts. and work 21 rows in double rib.
Increase row: Rib 4, up 1, rib 2, up 1, rib 11, ★ up 1, rib 2, (up 1, rib 15) 3 times ★; repeat from ★ to ★, up 1, rib 2, up 1, rib 11, up 1, rib 10, up 1, rib 2, up 1, rib 4. [155 sts.]
Change to size "A" needles and work as follows:
1st Foundation row: P.2, k.8, p.1, k.2, (p.1, k.1) 7 times, p.1, k.8, p.3, k.4, (p.1, k.1) 17 times, p.2, k.8, p.1, k.1, p.1, k.1, p.1, k.6, 3 from 1, k.2, p.1, k.1, p.1, k.1, m.k., k.1, p.1, k.1, p.1, k.2, 3 from 1, k.4, (p.1, k.1) 6 times, p.1, k.8, p.2, k.1, p.1, k.2, p.1, k.8, p.2.
2nd Foundation row (as 96th pattern row): P.1, k.1, p.8, k.1, (p.1, k.1) 3 times, p.8, k.2, (p.1, k.1) 5 times, p.5, ★ p.3 (these 3 sts. are represented by one square of the chart), p.3, k.1, (p.1, k.1) 3 times, p.3, p. the 3 sts. shown in one square of the chart, p.10, k.1, p.8, (k.1, p.1) 17 times, k.2, p.4, k.1★, p.1, k.1, p.8, k.2, (p.1, k.1) 8 times, p.8, k.1, p.1.
The last 2 rows set the position of the pattern given in the chart. Now work the 1st to 96th rows from the chart, then work the first 42 rows again.
★★Mark each end of the last row with colored threads to denote armholes. Pattern 64 rows.
To slope the shoulders: Noting the information given in the special note, bind off 57 sts. at the beginning of the next row, then working p.3tog. across the 2 groups of 3 sts. each shown in one square of the chart, bind off 57 sts. at the beginning and inc. 1 st. at the end of the following row. [42 sts.]
Back collar: Change to size "B" needles and work 16 rows in double rib. K. 4 rows, then p. 1 row and bind off loosely.

Front
Work as given for back until the armholes have been marked.
★★Pattern 41 rows. Now divide the sts. for the neck:
Next row: Pattern 67 and leave these sts. on a spare needle until required for right front shoulder, pattern 21 and leave these sts. on a stitch holder until required for collar, pattern to end and continue on these sts. for the left front shoulder.
Left front shoulder: To shape the neck: dec. 1 st. at the neck edge on each of the next 10 rows.
Pattern 12 rows, then bind off the remaining 57 sts.
Right front shoulder: With right side of work facing, rejoin yarn to the inner edge of the 67 sts. left on spare needle and work to end of row, then work as given for left front shoulder to end.
Collar: With right side of work facing rejoin yarn to left front shoulder and using size "B" needles, pick up and k. 20 sts. from left front neck edge, k. across the 21 sts. from stitch holder at center front neck, then pick up and k. 21 sts. from right front neck edge. [62 sts.]
Work 15 rows in double rib, then k. 4 rows and p. 1 row, then bind off loosely.

Sleeves
Both alike: With size "B" needles cast on 56 sts. and p. 1 row, then k. 4 rows. Now work 15 rows in double rib.
Increase row: Rib 6, ★ up 1, rib 2; repeat from ★ ending last repeat rib 6. [79 sts.]
Continuing with size "B" needles work in pattern as follows:
1st Foundation row: P.1, k.4, (p.1, k.1) 17 times, p.2, k.8, p.1, k.1, p.1, k.1, p.1, k.6, 3 from 1, k.2, p.1, k.1, p.1, k.1, m.k., k.1, p.1, k.1, p.1, k.2, 3 from 1, k.4.
2nd Foundation row (see 96th row on chart): P.4, then work as given for 2nd Foundation row on back from ★ to ★.
The last 2 rows set the position of the pattern given at the center of the chart, between the 2 lines.
Change to size "A" needles and work the first 44 pattern rows from the chart as set.
Now continuing in pattern as set and working the extra sts. in the moss st. background pattern as they occur, inc. 1 st. at each end of the next row and then every 6th row 8 times.
On 97 sts. pattern 23 rows for the woman's sweater or 39 rows for the man's.
To shape the sleeve top: Continuing in pattern as set, bind off 8 sts. at the beginning of the next 10 rows. Bind off the remaining 17 sts.

Making Up
Do not press. Join shoulder seams. Set in the sleeves, between the marking threads on back and front. Join sleeve and side seams.

S h o r t   S w e a t e r   P a t t e r n

Tension

12 stitches and 17 rows to 2 in (5 cm) over the moss stitch, using size "A" needles. Worked at this tension over the moss stitch, the 155 stitches across the back will measure 21 in (52.5 cm) in width and 96 rows – 1 repeat – of the pattern will measure 11¼ in (28 cm) in depth.

Measurements

Underarms: 42 in (105 cm). Side seam: 10½ in (26 cm). Length: 18¼ in (46 cm). Sleeve seam: 17 in (42.5 cm).

Back

With size "B" needles cast on 140 sts. and work 17 rows in double rib.
Work as given for back of Long Sweater from the increase row until the 72nd pattern row has been worked. Then continue as given for back from ★★ to end.

Front

Work as given for back until the armholes have been marked, then work as given for front of Long Sweater from ★★ to end.

Sleeves

Both alike: Work as given for sleeves on Long Sweater, but working 31 rows instead of 23 before shaping the sleeve top.

Making Up

As for Long Sweater.

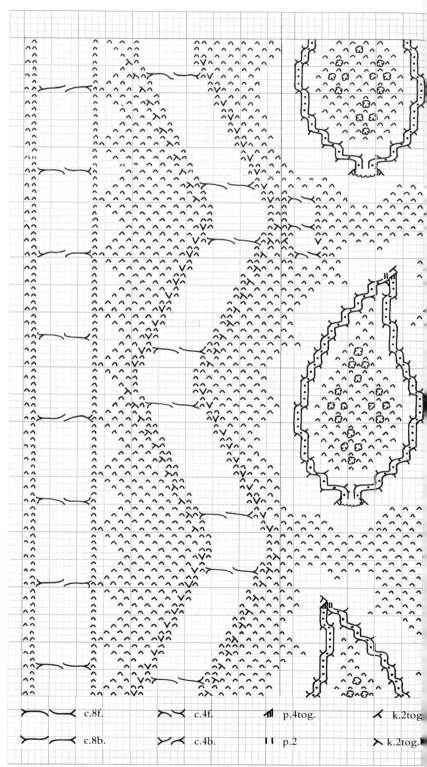

c.8f.   c.4f.   p.4tog.   k.2tog

c.8b.   c.4b.   p.2   k.2tog.

SLEEVE →

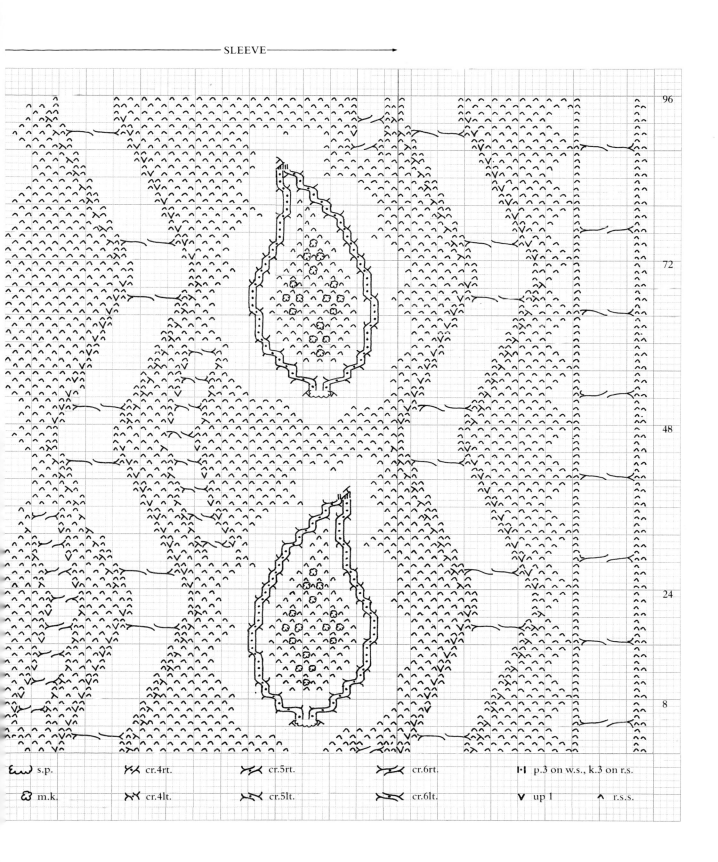

| 96 |
| 72 |
| 48 |
| 24 |
| 8 |

| ℰ | s.p. | ⅄⅄ | cr.4rt. | ⅄ | cr.5rt. | ⅄ | cr.6rt. | ⊢ | p.3 on w.s., k.3 on r.s. |
| ℬ | m.k. | ⅄⅄ | cr.4lt. | ⅄ | cr.5lt. | ⅄ | cr.6lt. | V | up 1 | ∧ | r.s.s. |

p a r r o t s

Strong colors suit this bold design which combines floral and parrot motifs with a moss stitch background.

SUMMER

Parrots Cardigan

PHOTOGRAPH THIS PAGE

Materials
10 50 gram balls of "Patricia Roberts Cotton No. 2" in main color and 1 ball of the same yarn in contrast color c.; plus 1 50 gram ball of "Patricia Roberts Extra Thick Cotton" in contrasts a., b. and d. and 2 balls of this yarn in each of the contrasts e. and f. A pair each of size 3 and size 5 Aero knitting needles, a medium-size cable needle and 5 buttons.

Colors
m. = yellow, a. = sand, b. = coral, c. = shocking pink, d. = olive, e. = red, f. = mauve.

Needle Sizes
Use size 5 needles for those referred to as size "A" in the pattern and size 3 needles for those referred to as size "B" in the pattern.

Abbreviations
c.8, cable 8 thus, slip next 4 sts. onto cable needle and leave at front of work, k. 4, then k. 4 from cable needle   **m.k.**, make knot thus, on right side rows k. 1, then slip this st. onto left-hand needle and p. the st., on wrong side rows p.1, then slip this st. onto left-hand needle and k. the st.

Tension
12 stitches and 16 rows to 2 in (5 cm) over the pattern using size "A" needles.

Cardigan Pattern

Measurements
Underarms: 47 in (117.5 cm). Side seam: 14¼ in (36 cm).

SUMMER

Parrots Cardigan
RIGHT

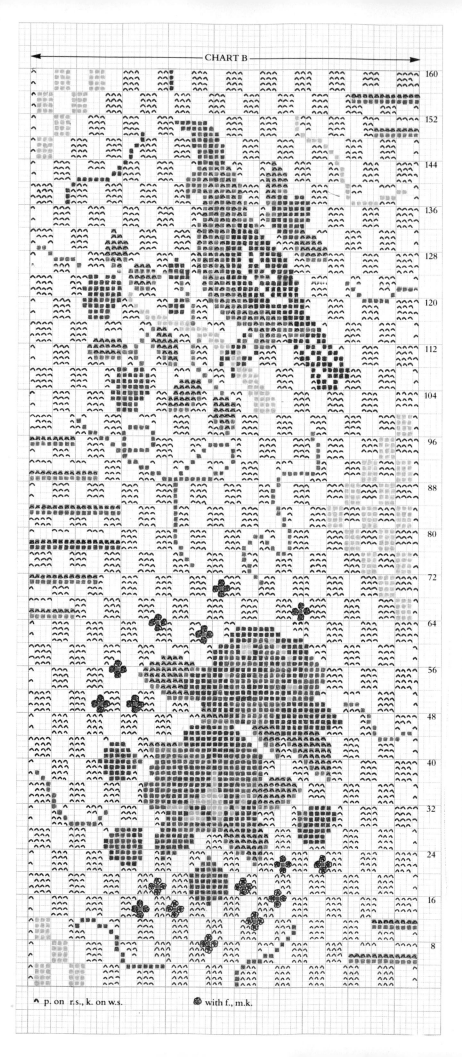

160
152
144
136
128
120
112
104
96
88
80
72
64
56
48
40
32
24
16
8

^ p. on r.s., k. on w.s. ⊛ with f., m.k.

Length: 22½ in (56 cm). Sleeve seam: 17 in (42.5 cm).

Back

With size "B" needles and m. cast on 118 sts. and work 19 rows in single rib.

Now divide the sts. for the left and right half and center back panels, for easier working, as follows:

Next row: Rib 6, up 1, (rib 4, up 1) 11 times, rib 4, inc. into next st. and leave these 68 sts. on a spare needle for left half back, inc., (rib 2, up 1) twice, rib 2, inc. and leave these 12 sts. on a stitch holder for the center panel, inc., (rib 4, up 1) 12 times, rib 6 and continue on these 68 sts. for right half back.

Right half back: Change to size "A" needles and work from chart A as follows: Use separate small balls of color for each motif and separate balls of m. at each side of the larger motifs, so that colors not in use are not taken across the back of work.

1st row: With m. k.4, (with a. k.3, with m. k.3) twice, with m. p.3, k.3, p.2, with b. k.1, with m. (k.3, p.3) twice, k.3, p.2, with c. k.1, with m. (k.3, p.3) 4 times, k.1.

2nd row: With m. k.4, (p.3, k.3) 3 times, p.3, with c. p.1, with m. k.2, (p.3, k.3) twice, p.2, with b. p.1, with m. p.1, k.2, p.3, k.3, p.3, with a. p.3, with m. p.3, with a. p.3, with m. p.3, k.1.

The last 2 rows set the position of the pattern given in Chart A.

Work the 3rd to 94th rows from the chart. Mark the end of the last row with a colored thread to denote armhole.

Work the 95th to 156th pattern rows from the chart.

To slope the shoulder: Bind off 22 sts. at the beginning of the next row and the following alternate row. On 24sts. work 1 row, then bind off loosely.

Left half back: With right side of work facing, rejoin yarn to the inner edge of the 68 sts. left on the spare needle and using size "A" needles, work in pattern as follows:

1st row: With m. k.4, (p.3, k.3) 4 times, p.3, with f. k.1, with m. k.2, (p.3, k.3) 4 times, with a. k.3, with m. k.3, with a. k.3, with m. k.1.

2nd row: With m. k.1, with a. p.3, with m. p.3, with a. p.3, with m. (p.3, k.3) 4 times, p.2, with f. p.1, with m. (k.3, p.3) 5 times, k.1.

The last 2 rows set the position of the pattern given in Chart B.

Work the 3rd to 95th rows from the chart. Mark the end of the last row with a colored thread to denote armhole.

Work the 96th to 157th rows.

To slope the shoulder: Bind off 22 sts. at the beginning of the next row and the following alternate row. Bind off the remaining 24 sts. loosely.

Center panel: With right side of work facing rejoin m. to the 12 sts. left on stitch holder and using size "A" needles work as follows:

1st row: All k.

2nd row: K.2, p.8, k.2.

3rd to 6th rows: Repeat 1st and 2nd rows twice.

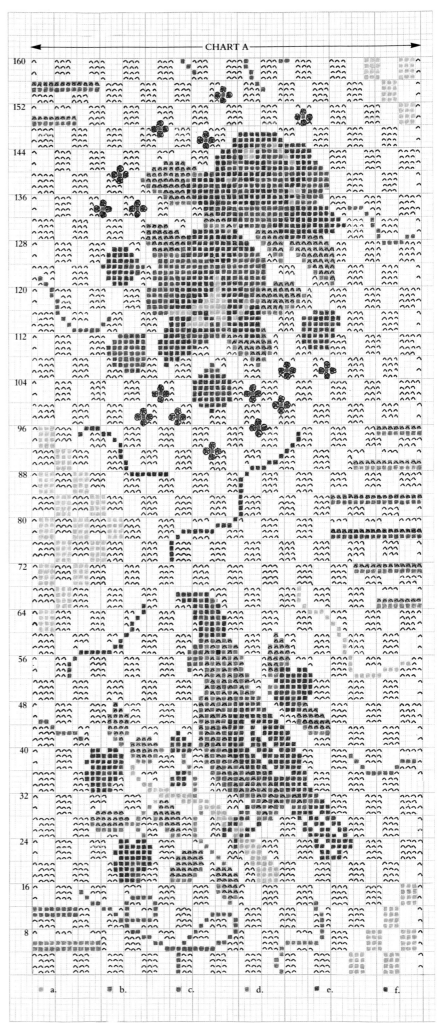

CHART A

7th row: K.2, c.8, k.2.

8th row: As 2nd row.

9th to 12th rows: Repeat 1st and 2nd rows twice.

These 12 rows form the cable pattern. Repeat them 12 times more, then bind off.

Neatly sew cable panel in place at center back, joining it to edges of left and right half back panels.

Left Front

With size "B" needles and m. cast on 56 sts. and work 19 rows in single rib.

Increase row: Rib 6, ★ up 1, rib 4; repeat from ★ ending last repeat rib 6. [68 sts.]

Change to size "A" needles and work the 1st to 94th rows from the chart as given for right half back. Mark the end of the last row with a colored thread to denote armhole.

★★ **To slope the front edge:** Dec. 1 st. at the end of the next row and the 23 following alternate rows. On 44 sts. pattern 15 rows.

To slope the shoulder: Bind off 22 sts. at the

beginning of the next row. On 22 sts. work 1 row, then bind off.

Right Front

Work as given for left front until the increase row has been worked.

Change to size "A" needles and work the 1st to 95th rows from the chart as given for left half back. Mark the end of the last row with a colored thread to denote armhole.

To slope the front edge: Work as given for left front from ★★ to end.

Frontband: First join shoulder seams. With size "B" needles and m. cast on 10 sts. and k. 8 rows.

1st Buttonhole row: K.3, bind off 4, k. to end.

2nd Buttonhole row: K.3, turn, cast on 4 over those bound off, turn, k. to end.

K. 28 rows.

Repeat the last 30 rows 3 times more, then work the 2 buttonhole rows again.

Continue in garter stitch until the band is long enough to fit up right front, with the last buttonhole in line with the first front edge dec., around neck edge and down left front.

Sew in place and bind off, when correct length is assured.

Pocket backs (Both alike): With size "A" needles and m. cast on 30 sts. and work in stripes as follows:

With m. k. 4 rows, then with a. beginning with a k. row, s.s. 4 rows.

Repeat these 8 rows 4 times more.

With m. k. 4 rows, then bind off.

Sleeves

Both alike: With size "B" needles and m. cast on 56 sts. and work 19 rows in single rib.

Increase row: Rib 6, ★ up 1, rib 4; repeat from ★ ending last repeat rib 6. [68 sts.]

Change to size "A" needles and work the 1st to 60th pattern rows, as given for left half back.

Continuing in pattern and working the extra sts. into the background basket st. pattern as they occur, inc. 1 st. at each end of the next row and the 19 following alternate rows.

On 108 sts. pattern 17 rows, then bind off loosely.

Making Up

Do not press. Sew bound off edges of sleeves to the straight row ends between the marking threads on back and front. Join sleeve and side seams, neatly sewing pocket backs in place in side seams and to back of fronts. Sew on buttons.

summer *variations*

Tea Rose T-shirt

ABOVE LEFT
Bright red roses sing out against a dazzling white background on this fresh and summery cotton T-shirt.
PATTERN PAGE 152

Kashmir Vest

BELOW LEFT
Rich lurex yarn worked into this design creates the effect of a sprinkling of gold dust.
PATTERN PAGE 42

Long Raj Cardigan

RIGHT
Cool white cotton makes this long version of the Indian-inspired Raj design perfect for summer heat.
PATTERN PAGE 142

l i l a c s

Based on delicate lilac blossoms, this design for a sweater and a cardigan is knitted in cotton or wool. It can encompass a range of colors, from cool pastels and sultry summer hues to dramatic blacks and reds for winter.

S U M M E R

L i l a c s   S w e a t e r

PHOTOGRAPH THIS PAGE

Materials
14 50 gram balls of "Patricia Roberts Cotton No.2" in main color and for the contrast colors in "Patricia Roberts Extra Thick Cotton" in 50 gram balls – 3 balls in color b., 2 balls in color d., and 1 ball in color e. In this version, a. and c. are worked in the same color so a total of 2 balls will be required. A pair each of size 3 and size 5 Aero knitting needles.

Colors
m. = white, a. and c. = lilac, b. = soft pink, d. = mustard, e. = olive.

Needle Sizes
Use size 5 needles for those referred to as size "A" in the pattern and size 3 needles for those referred to as size "B" in the pattern.

S U M M E R

L i l a c s   C a r d i g a n

PHOTOGRAPH THIS PAGE

Materials
14 50 gram balls of "Patricia Roberts Cotton No.2" in main color and in the contrast colors in "Patricia Roberts Extra Thick Cotton" in 50 gram balls – 3 balls in color b., 2 balls in color d. and 1 ball in color e. In this version, a. and c. are worked in the same color so a total of 2 balls will be required. A pair each of size 5 and size 3 Aero knitting needles; 8 buttons.

Colors
m. = lilac, a. and c. = navy, b. = orient blue, d. = mustard, e. = olive.

S U M M E R

Lilacs Sweater
ABOVE RIGHT,
BELOW RIGHT
AND OPPOSITE

Lilacs Cardigan
CENTER RIGHT

A U T U M N

Lilacs Sweater
PAGE 99

Needle Sizes

Use size 5 needles for those referred to as size "A" and size 3 for those referred to as size "B" in the pattern.

AUTUMN

Lilacs Sweater

PHOTOGRAPH PAGE 99

Materials

14 50 gram balls of "Patricia Roberts Pure Wool No.2" in main color and for the contrast colors in "Patricia Roberts Extra Thick Wool" in 100 gram balls – 2 balls in color b. and 1 ball in each of the contrasts a., c., d. and e. A pair each of size 3 and size 6 Aero knitting needles.

Colors

m. = black, a. = plum, b. = shocking pink, c. = red, d. = khaki, e. = olive.

Needle Sizes

Use size 6 needles for those referred to as size "A" in the pattern and size 3 needles for those referred to as size "B" in the pattern.

Abbreviations

m.h.b., make half bobble thus, with a. k. into front and back of next st., turn, p.2, turn, k.2 ■ **m.k.**, make knot thus, on right side rows: k.1, slip st. just made onto left-hand needle and p. this st.; on wrong side rows: work p. instead of k. and k. instead of p.

Tension

12 stitches and 16 rows to 2 in (5 cm) over stockinette stitch using size "A" needles.

Sweater Pattern

Measurements

Underarms: 48 in (120 cm). Side seam: 17¼ in (43 cm). Length: 26¾ in (67 cm). Sleeve seam: 17 in (42.5 cm).

Back

With size "B" needles and m. cast on 132 sts. and work 19 rows in double rib.
Increase row: Rib 5, ★ up 1, rib 11; repeat from ★

ending last repeat rib 6. [144 sts.]
Change to size "A" needles and work the border pattern as follows:
1st to 4th rows: With m. all k.
5th row: ★ With m. k.2, with b. k.2; repeat from ★ to end.
6th row: ★ With b. p.2, with m. p.2; repeat from ★ to end.
7th row: ★ With b. k.2, with m. k.2; repeat from ★ to end.
8th row: ★ With m. p.2, with b. p.2; repeat from ★ to end.
9th to 12th rows: With m. all k.
With m. beginning with a k. row, s.s. 2 rows. Now work in main pattern as follows: Use separate small balls of contrast colors for each section of the motifs so that colors not in use are not taken across the back of the work.
1st row: Work across part A of the chart as follows:
★ With d. k. 5, with m. k. 31, with a. m.h.b., with m. k.11 ★. Now work across part B of the chart as follows: With m. k.47, with d. k.1; then work across part A of the chart again from ★ to ★.
2nd row: Working back ★ across chart A: With m. p. 11, p.2tog., p.30, with d. p.1, with m. p.5 ★; then across chart B with m. p.1, with d. p.1, with m. p.46; repeat from ★ to ★.
The last 2 rows set the position of the pattern, work the 3rd to 52nd rows as set.
For the next repeat of the pattern parts A and B of the chart are transposed, so work as follows:
1st row: ★ Work across chart B thus: With m. k.47, with d. k.1 ★; then across part A thus: With d. k.5, with m. k.31, with a. m.h.b., with m. k.11; repeat from ★ to ★.
2nd row: ★ Work back across chart B thus: With m. p.1, with d. p.1, with m. p.46 ★; across chart A thus: With m. p.11, p.2tog., p.30, with d. p.1, with m. p.5; repeat from ★ to ★.
The last 2 rows set the position of parts A and B of the chart, work the 3rd to 52nd rows from the chart as set. Mark each end of the last row with colored threads to denote armholes.★★ Now work the first repeat of the pattern again. This completes the main pattern.
Work the 1st to 8th rows of the border pattern, then work the 1st to 12th rows.
To slope the shoulders: Working in s.s. with m., bind off 24 sts. at the beginning of the next 4 rows. Bind off the remaining 48 sts. loosely.

Front

Work as given for back until ★★ is reached, but

working as given for the second repeat of the pattern first, then as given for the first repeat.

Now work the first 47 rows of the second repeat of the pattern again.

Now divide the sts. for the neck:

Next row: Pattern 60 and leave these sts. on a spare needle until required for right front shoulder, bind off 24 sts. for the neck, pattern to end and continue on these 60 sts. for the left front shoulder.

Left front shoulder: To shape the neck, dec. 1 st. at the neck edge on each of the next 4 rows. This completes the main pattern.

Still decreasing 1 st. at the neck edge on each row, work the first 8 rows of the border pattern.

On 48 sts. work the 1st to 12th rows of the border pattern. ★★★

To slope the shoulder: Working in s.s. with m. bind off 24 sts. at the beginning of the next row. On 24 sts. work 1 row, then bind off.

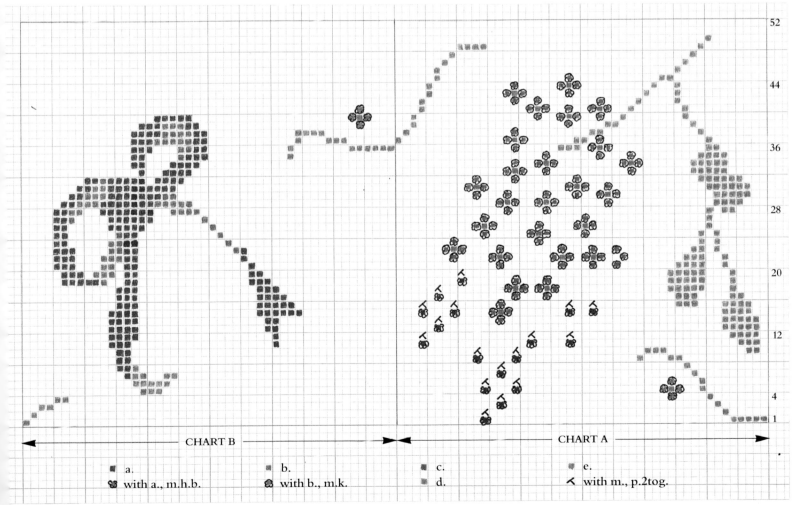

■ a.	■ b.	■ c.	▮ e.	
⊠ with a., m.h.b.	⊗ with b., m.k.	▤ d.	⟨ with m., p.2tog.	

CHART B ◀━━━━━━━━━━━━━━━━━▶◀━━━━━━━━ CHART A ━━━━━━━━━▶

Right front shoulder: With right side of work facing rejoin yarn to inner edge of sts. left on spare needle and work as given for left front shoulder until ★★★ is reached. With m. k. 1 row, then work as given for left front shoulder.

Neckband: First join right shoulder seam, then with right side of work facing, rejoin m. to left front shoulder and using size "B" needles, pick up and k. 27 sts. from left front neck edge, 24 sts. from center front neck, 27 sts. from right front neck edge, then 48 sts. from back neck edge.
On 126 sts. work 9 rows in double rib, then bind off in rib.

Sleeves
Both alike: With size "B" needles cast on 48 sts. and work 15 rows in double rib.
Increase row: Rib 1, ★ up 1, rib 2; repeat from ★ ending last repeat rib 1. [72 sts.]
Change to size "A" needles and work the 12 row border pattern.
Increase row: K.1, ★ up 1, k.3; repeat from ★ ending last repeat k.2. [96 sts.]
With m. p. 1 row.
Now work in main pattern as follows:
1st row: Work across the 48 sts. of part A of the chart, then across the 48 sts. of part B.
2nd row: Work back across the sts. of part B of the chart then back across those of part A.
Work the 3rd to 52nd rows from the chart as set. For the next repeat of the pattern work as follows:
1st row: Work across the 48 sts. of part B of the chart, then work across the 48 sts. of part A.
2nd row: Work back across the 48 sts. of part A of the chart, then work back across the 48 sts. of part B.
Maintaining the continuity of the pattern as set, inc. 1 st. at each end of the next row and then every 6th row 8 times.
On 114 sts. pattern 3 rows. Bind off loosely.

Making Up
Do not press. Join shoulder seams. Sew bound off edges of sleeves to the straight row ends between the marking threads on back and front. Join sleeve and side seams.

Cardigan Pattern

Measurements
Underarms: 49 in (123 cm). Side seam: 17¼ in (43 cm). Length: 26¾ in (67 cm). Sleeve seam: 17 in (42.5 cm).

Back
Work as given for Sweater Pattern.

Left Front
With size "B" needles and m. cast on 66 sts. and work 19 rows in double rib.
Increase row: Rib 5, ★ up 1, rib 11; repeat from ★ ending last repeat rib 6. [72 sts.]
Change to size "A" needles and work as given for back until the main pattern is reached.
1st row: ★ Work across part B of the chart thus: With m. k.47, with d. k.1 ★; then across part A of the chart thus: With d. k.5, with m. k.19.
2nd row: ★ Work back across part A thus. With m p.18, with d. p.1, with m. p.5; then across part B thus: With m. p.1, with d. p.1, with m. p.46.
The last 2 rows set the position of parts A and B of the chart. Work the 3rd to 52nd rows from the chart as set. For the next repeat of the pattern parts A and B of the chart are transposed, so work as follows:
1st row: Work across part A thus: With d. k.5, with m. k.31, with a. m.h.b., with m. k.11; across part B thus: With m. k.24.
2nd row: Work back across part B thus: With m. p.24, then across part A thus: With m. p.11, p.2tog., p.30, with d. p.1, with m. p.5.
The last 2 rows set the position of parts A and B of the chart. Work the 3rd to 52nd rows from the chart as set. Mark the end of the last row with a colored thread to denote armhole.
Now work the first 47 rows of the next repeat of the pattern.
To shape the neck: Bind off 12 sts. at the beginning of the next row, then dec. 1 st. at the neck edge on each of the next 4 rows. This completes the main pattern. Still decreasing 1 st. at the neck edge on each row, work the first 8 rows of the border pattern.
On 48 sts. work the 1st to 12th rows of the border pattern.
To slope the shoulder: Working in s.s. with m. bind off 24 sts. at the beginning of the next row. On 24 sts. work 1 row, then bind off.
Buttonband: With size "B" needles and m. cast on 9 sts. and work 196 rows in single rib, then bind off.

Right Front
Work as given for left front until the main pattern is reached.
1st row: Work across part A of the chart as follows: With m. k.12, with a. m.h.b., with m. k.11. Now work across part B of the chart as follows: With m. k.47, with d. k.1.

2nd row: Working back across part B of the chart with m. p.1, with d. p.1, with m. p.46; then work back across part A: With m. p. 11, p.2tog., p.12.

The last 2 rows set the position of the pattern. Work the 3rd to 52nd rows as set.

For the next repeat of the pattern parts A and B of the chart are transposed, so work as follows:

1st row: Work across part B thus: With m. k.23, with d. k.1; then across part A thus: With d. k.5, with m. k.31, with a. m.h.b., with m. k.11.

2nd row: Work across part A thus: With m. p.11, p.2tog., p.30, with d. p.1, with m. p.5; then across part B thus: With m. p.1, with d. p.1, with m. p. to end.

The last 2 rows set the position of parts A and B of the chart. Work the 3rd to 52nd rows from the chart as set. Mark the beginning of the last row with colored threads to denote armhole.

Now work the first 48 rows of the next repeat of the pattern.

To shape the neck: Bind off 12 sts. at the beginning of the next row, then dec. 1 st. at the neck edge on each of the next 3 rows. Still decreasing at neck edge on each row, work the first 8 rows of the border pattern, then the first row again.

On 48 sts. work the 2nd to 12th rows of border pattern, then k. 1 row.

To slope the shoulder: Work as given for left front.

Buttonhole band: With size "B" needles and m. cast on 9 sts. and work 8 rows in single rib.

1st Buttonhole row: Rib 3, bind off 3, rib to end.

2nd Buttonhole row: Rib 3, turn, cast on 3, turn, rib to end.

Rib 24 rows.

Repeat the last 26 rows 6 times more, then work the 2 buttonhole rows again.

Rib 4 rows, then bind off.

Neckband: First join shoulder seams, then with right side of work facing, rejoin m. to right front neck edge and using size "B" needles, pick up and k. 39 sts. from right front neck edge, 48 sts. from back neck edge and 39 sts. from left front neck edge.

On 126 sts. work 9 rows in double rib. Bind off in rib.

Sleeves

As given for Sweater Pattern.

Making Up

Do not press. Sew bound off edges of sleeves to the straight row ends between the marking threads on back and front. Join sleeve and side seams. Neatly sew frontbands in place. Sew on buttons.

b o b b l e s

The hood adds a distinctive touch to this versatile one-color jacket with its raised patterning of bobbles. Knitted in Extra Thick Cotton for summer and Extra Thick Wool for autumn and winter, it can be light enough to pull on for a balmy summer evening or warm enough to take the place of a coat in the cooler months. In spite of the impressive effect, it is a straightforward design to knit.

S U M M E R

B o b b l e s   J a c k e t

PHOTOGRAPH THIS PAGE

Materials
22 50 gram balls of "Patricia Roberts Extra Thick Cotton." A pair each of size 5 and size 6 Aero knitting needles; 7 buttons.

Colors
Miami pink
or
aqua blue

Needle Sizes
Use size 5 needles for those referred to as size "B" in the pattern and size 6 needles for those referred to as size "A" in the pattern.

A U T U M N

B o b b l e s   J a c k e t

PHOTOGRAPH PAGE 98

Materials
11 100 gram balls of "Patricia Roberts Extra Thick Wool." A pair each of size 6 and size 7 Aero knitting needles; 7 buttons.

Color
Faded violet

Needle Sizes
Use size 6 needles for those referred to as size "B" in the pattern and size 7 needles for those referred to as size "A" in the pattern.

SUMMER

Bobbles Jacket
RIGHT

AUTUMN

Bobbles Jacket
PAGE 98

WINTER

Bobbles Jacket
PAGE 136

WINTER

B o b b l e s   J a c k e t

P H O T O G R A P H   P A G E   1 3 6

Materials
11 100 gram balls of "Patricia Roberts Extra Thick Wool." A pair of size 6 and size 7 Aero knitting needles; 7 buttons.

Color
Cream

Needle Sizes
Use size 6 needles for those referred to as size "B" in the pattern and size 7 needles for those referred to as size "A" in the pattern.

Abbreviations
m.b., make bobble thus, k. into back and front of st., turn, k.2, turn, p.2, turn, k.2, turn, k.2tog.

Tension
10 stitches and 14 rows to 2 in (5 cm) over stockinette stitch using size "A" needles.

J a c k e t   P a t t e r n

Measurements
Underarms: 54 in (135 cm). Side seam: 18 in (45 cm). Length: 28 in (70 cm). Sleeve seam: 17 in (43 cm).

Back
With size "A" needles cast on 144 sts. and work 6 rows in double rib.
K. 2 rows.
Work border pattern as follows:
1st row: K.3, ★ p.1, k.5; repeat from ★ ending last repeat k.2.
2nd row: P.1, ★ k.3, p.3; repeat from ★ ending last repeat p.2.
Work the 3rd to 12th rows from the chart.
Now work the main pattern as follows:
1st to 4th rows: In s.s.
5th row: K.15, ★ p.1, k.1, p.1, k.21; repeat from ★ ending last repeat k.6.
6th row: P.7, ★ k.1, p.1, k.1, p.21; repeat from ★ ending last repeat p.14.
Work the 7th to 48th rows from the chart.★★

Continuing in the 64 row repeat pattern, dec. 1 st. at each end of the next row and then every 12th row 4 times.
On 134 sts. pattern 9 rows.
To shape the armholes: Continuing in pattern, bind off 6 sts. at the beginning of the next 2 rows, then dec. 1 st. at each end of the next row and the 8 following alternate rows. [104 sts.] This completes the main pattern.
S.s. 2 rows.
Decrease row: P.5, ★ p.3tog., p.12; repeat from ★ ending last repeat, p.6. [90 sts.]
S.s. 2 rows, then work the 12 row border pattern. Repeat these 14 rows twice more.
To slope the shoulders: Continuing in s.s., bind off 8 sts. at the beginning of the next 6 rows.
Bind off the remaining 42 sts. loosely.

Left Front
Pocket backs: With size "A" needles, cast on 28 sts. and work 40 rows (41 rows on right front) in s.s. and leave on a stitch holder until required.
With size "A" needles cast on 72 sts. and work as given for back until ★★ is reached. Work 1 extra row here, when working right front.
Continuing in pattern dec. 1 st. at the beginning of the next row and the following 12th row.
Work 3 rows.
Pocket row: Pattern 8, slip next 28 sts. onto a stitch holder until required for pocket top and in their place pattern across the 28 sts. of pocket back, to work to end.
Continuing in pattern and decreasing 1 st. at side seam edge on every 12th row as set, work 41 rows. [67 sts.]
To shape the armholes: Bind off 6 sts. at the beginning of the next row, then dec. 1 st. at the same edge on the 9 following alternate rows. [52 sts.]
S.s. 2 rows. Work 1 row less on right front.
Decrease row: P.4, ★ p.3tog., p.7; repeat from ★ ending last repeat, p.5. [42 sts.]
S.s. 2 rows, then work the 12 row border pattern.
Continuing in this 14 row pattern, work 7 rows. Work 1 row more on right front.
To shape the neck: Bind off 6 sts. at the beginning of the next row, then dec. 1 st. at the same edge on each of the next 12 rows.
On 24 sts. work 8 rows.
To slope the shoulder: Bind off 8 sts. at the beginning of the next row and the following alternate row. On 8 sts. work 1 row, then bind off.
Pocket top: With right side of work facing, rejoin

yarn to the 28 sts. left on stitch holder and using size "B" needles work 6 rows in double rib, then bind off in rib.

Buttonband: With size "B" needles cast on 6 sts. and work 170 rows in single rib. Bind off in rib.

Right Front

Work as given for left front, noting the changes in the number of rows.

Pocket top: As given for left front.

Buttonhole band: With size "B" needles cast on 6 sts. and work 6 rows in single rib.

1st Buttonhole row: Rib 2, bind off 2, rib to end.

2nd Buttonhole row: Rib 2, turn, cast on 2 over those bound off, turn, rib 2.

Rib 24 rows. Repeat the last 26 rows 5 times, then work the 2 buttonhole rows again.

Rib 6 rows, then bind off.

Hood

Right half: With size "A" needles cast on 72 sts. and work as given for back until 24 rows have been worked in main pattern.

Dec. 1 st. at the beginning of the next row and then every 4th row 5 times, then at the same edge on the following 13 rows. Bind off loosely.

Left half: As given for right half, reversing the shaping.

Sleeves

Both alike: With size "B" needles cast on 40 sts. and work 11 rows in double rib.

Increase row: ★ Inc. in next st., rib 4; repeat from ★ to end. [48 sts.]

Change to size "A" needles and k. 2 rows, then work the 12 row border pattern given for back.

Work the first 26 rows of the main pattern.

Maintaining the continuity of the pattern as set and working the extra sts. into the pattern, inc. 1 st. at each end of the next row and then every 4th row 15 times.

On 80 sts. pattern 7 rows.

To shape the sleeve top: Bind off 6 sts. at the beginning of the next 2 rows, then dec. 1 st. at each end of the next row and the 8 following alternate rows, then at each end of the next 5 rows. Bind off 5 sts. at the beginning of the next 6 rows. Bind off the remaining 10 sts.

Making Up

Do not press. Join shoulder seams. Set in sleeves. Join sleeve and side seams. Sew button- and buttonhole bands in position. Join shaped row end and bound off edges of hood halves. Neatly sew other row end edges of hood in place all round neck edges, so that the ribbing is sewn to the top of button- and buttonhole bands. Neatly sew pocket backs and row ends of pocket tops in place. Sew on buttons.

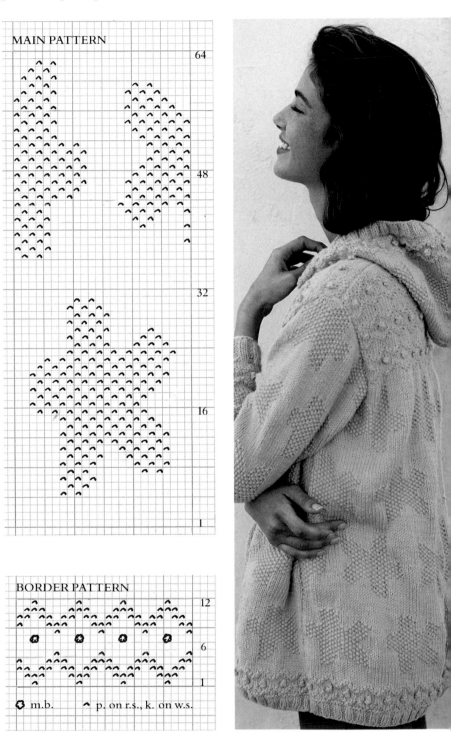

MAIN PATTERN

BORDER PATTERN

⊘ m.b.   ︿ p. on r.s., k. on w.s.

angel fish

Tropical angel fish make a bold splash among cheerful waves on this exotic design for both a sweater and a cardigan.

SUMMER

Angel Fish Sweater

PHOTOGRAPH THIS PAGE

Materials
10 50 gram balls of "Patricia Roberts Cotton No. 2" in main color and 8 50 gram balls of "Patricia Roberts Extra Thick Cotton" in contrast b. plus 1 ball of the same yarn in each of the contrasts a., c., d. and e. A pair each of size 5 and size 3 Aero knitting needles and a medium-size cable needle.

Colors
m. = white, a. = sand, b. = orient blue, c. = navy, d. = khaki, e. = aqua blue.

Needle Sizes
Use size 5 needles for those referred to as size "A" and size 3 needles for those referred to as size "B" in the pattern.

SUMMER

Angel Fish Cardigan

PHOTOGRAPH THIS PAGE

Materials
11 50 gram balls of "Patricia Roberts Cotton No. 2" in main color and 8 50 gram balls of "Patricia Roberts Extra Thick Cotton" in contrast b., plus 1 ball in each of the contrasts a., c., d. and e. A pair each of size 5 and size 3 Aero knitting needles, a medium-size cable needle and 7 buttons.

Colors
m. = aqua, a. = white, b. = orient blue for the border pattern and navy for the chart pattern, c. = orient blue, d. = khaki, e. = sand.

Needle Sizes
Use size 5 needles for those referred to as size "A" and

SUMMER

Angel Fish Sweater

CENTER RIGHT

Angel Fish Cardigan

ABOVE RIGHT, BELOW RIGHT AND OPPOSITE

AUTUMN

Angel Fish Sweater

PAGE 119

size 3 needles for those referred to as size "B" in the pattern.

AUTUMN

Angel Fish Sweater

PHOTOGRAPH PAGE 119

Materials

10 50 gram balls of "Patricia Roberts Pure Wool No. 2" in main color and 4 100 gram balls of "Patricia Roberts Extra Thick Wool" in contrast b., plus 1 ball of the same yarn in each of the contrasts a., c., d. and e. A pair each of size 6 and size 3 Aero knitting needles and a medium-size cable needle.

Colors

m. = airforce blue, a. = khaki, b. = navy blue, c. = faded violet, d. = olive, e. = royal blue.

Needle Sizes

Use size 6 needles for those referred to as size "A" and size 3 needles for those referred to as size "B" in the pattern.

Abbreviations

h.b., half bobble thus, k. into back and front of next st., turn, k.2, turn, p.2 ■ **s.c.,** start circle thus, with a. k.1, y.r.n., k.1, y.r.n., k.1 all into same st., turn, p.5, turn, k.5 ■ **cr.3rt.,** cross 3 right thus, slip next st. onto cable needle at back of work, with a. k.2, with m. k.1 from cable needle ■ **cr.3lt.,** cross 3 left thus, slip next 2 sts. onto cable needle at front of work, with m. k.1, with a. k.2 from cable needle ■ **4 onto 1,** thus, slip next 3 sts. onto left-hand needle, pass 2nd st. on left-hand needle over first st., ★ slip this st. back to other needle and pass the 2nd st. over it; repeat from ★ twice more, with m. p. the remaining st.

Tension

The tension is based on a stockinette stitch tension of 12 stitches and 16 rows to 2 in (5 cm) using size "A" needles.

Sweater Pattern

Measurements

Underarms: 48 in (120 cm). Side seam: 17¼ in (43 cm). Length: 26½ in (66 cm). Sleeve seam: 17 in (42.5 cm).

Back

With size "B" needles and m. cast on 121 sts. and work 17 rows in single rib.

Increase row: Rib 3, ★ up 1, rib 5; repeat from ★ ending last repeat rib 3. [145 sts.]

Change to size "A" needles and work the border pattern as follows:

1st and 2nd rows: With b. all k.

3rd row: With m. all k.

4th row: With m. all p.

5th row: With m. k.3, ★ with b. h.b., with m. k.3; repeat from ★ ending last repeat k.1.

6th row: With m. p.1, ★ slip next 2 sts. onto cable needle at back of work, with m. p.2, with b. k.2 from cable needle, with m. p.1; repeat from ★ to end.

7th row: With m. k.1, ★ s.s.k., k.3; repeat from ★ to end.

8th row: With m. all p.

9th and 10th rows: With b. all k.

11th row: With m. all k.

12th row: With m. p.4, ★ with b. p.1, with m. p.7; repeat from ★ ending last repeat with m. p.4.

13th row: With m. k.3, ★ with b. k.1, p.1, k.1, with m. k.5; repeat from ★ ending last repeat with m. k.3.

14th row: With m. p.2, ★ with b. p.1, k.3, p.1, with m. p.3; repeat from ★ ending last repeat with m. p.2.

15th row: With m. k.1, ★ with b. k.1, p.5, k.1, with m. k.1; repeat from ★ to end.

16th row: With b. p.1, ★ k.7, p.1; repeat from ★ to end.

17th and 18th rows: With b. all k.

The last 18 rows form the border pattern. Repeat them once more.

With m. k. 1 row.

Now work the fish pattern as follows:

Foundation row: With m. k.1, up 1, k.3, ★ p.6, k.6; repeat from ★ ending last repeat k.2, up 1, inc. [148 sts.] ★★

Now work the 1st to 82nd pattern rows given in the chart, marking each end of the last row with colored threads to denote armholes.

On 145 sts. work the yoke pattern as follows:

1st to 18th rows: As given for border pattern.

19th row: With m. all k.

20th row: With m. p.1, ★ p.3tog., p.2, up 1 p.wise (by picking up the loop between the needles, slipping it onto left-hand needle and purling into **back** of it), p.1, up 1 p.wise, p.2, up 1 p.wise, p.1, up 1 p.wise, p.2, p.3tog., p.2; repeat from ★ to end.

21st and 22nd rows: As 19th and 20th rows.

23rd to 26th rows: With b. all k.

27th to 34th rows: As 19th to 26th rows.

35th to 42nd rows: As 19th to 26th rows.

43rd to 50th rows: As 19th to 26th rows.

51st row: As 15th row.

52nd row: As 14th row.

53rd row: As 13th row.

54th row: As 12th row.

55th row: With m. all k.

56th row: With m. all p.

Now work the 1st to 10th rows again.

To slope the shoulders: Working in s.s. with m.

only, bind off 12 sts. at the beginning of the next 8 rows. [49 sts.]

Neckband: Change to size "B" needles and with m. work 8 rows in single rib, then bind off in rib.

Front

Work as given for back until the first 49 rows of the yoke pattern have been worked.

Now divide the sts. for the neck:

Next row: With b. k.61 and leave these sts. on a spare needle until required for right front shoulder, k.23 and leave these sts. on stitch holder until required for neckband, k. to end and continue on these 61 sts. for the left front shoulder.

Left front shoulder: To shape the neck, dec. 1 st at the neck edge on the next 13 rows.

On 48 sts. work 3 rows. ★★★

To slope the shoulder: Continuing with m. in s.s., bind off 12 sts. at the beginning of the next row and the 2 following alternate rows. On 12 sts. work 1 row, then bind off.

Right front shoulder: With right side of work facing rejoin yarn to inner edge of sts. left on spare needle and work as given for left front shoulder until ★★★ is reached.

With m. k.1 row, then slope the shoulder as given for left front shoulder.

Neckband: With right side of work facing rejoin m. and using size "B" needles pick up and k. 24 sts. from left front neck edge, k. across the 23 sts. at center front, then pick up and k. 24 sts. from right front neck edge. On 71 sts. work 7 rows in single rib, then bind off in rib.

Sleeves

Both alike: With size "B" needles and m. cast on 51 sts. and work 23 rows in single rib.

Increase row: Rib 1, ★ up 1, rib 4; repeat from ★ until 2 remain, up 1, rib 1, inc. [65 sts.]

Change to size "A" needles and work the first 16 rows of the yoke pattern given for back.

Continuing in yoke pattern as a repeat pattern, and working the extra sts. into the pattern as they occur, inc. 1 st. at each end of the next row and then every 6th row 15 times.

On 97 sts. pattern 5 rows, then bind off loosely.

Making Up

Do not press. Join shoulder seams. Sew bound off edges of sleeves to the straight row ends between the marking threads on back and front. Join sleeve and side seams.

C a r d i g a n   P a t t e r n

M e a s u r e m e n t s

Underarms: 49 in (122.5 cm). Side seam: 17¼ in
(43 cm).
Length: 26½ in (66 cm). Sleeve seam: 17 in (42.5 cm).

B a c k

Work as given for back of Sweater Pattern.

L e f t   F r o n t

With size "B" needles and m. cast on 61 sts. and work
as given for back until the 18-row border pattern has

| **V** up 1 | **⅄** s.s.k. | **⅄** k.2tog. | **⋀** 4 onto 1 | **⋊⋉** cr.3lt. | **⋊⋉** cr.3rt. | **‖** with a., p.2 on w.s. | **⊗** s.c. |

⋀ r.s.s.

been worked twice, noting that there are 73 sts. after working the increase row.

With m. k. 1 row, increasing 1 st. at end. [74 sts.] ★★

Now work the fish pattern as follows:

Foundation row: With m. k.3, ★ p.6, k.6; repeat from ★ ending last repeat k.5.

80

72

64

56

48

40

32

24

16

8

■ a.   ■ b.   ■ c.   ■ d.   ■ e.

1st row: With m. k.1, (p.2, k.4) 9 times, p.2, k.2, with a. k.2, with m. p.2, k.4, p.2, k.4, p.1.
2nd row: With m. p.3, k.3, with a. p.2, with m. k.1, p.3, with a. p.3, with m. (k.6, p.6) 4 times, k.6, p.5. The last 2 rows set the position of the pattern given on the right-hand side of the chart. Now work the 3rd to 82nd rows from the chart. Mark the end of the last row with a colored thread to denote armhole. [73 sts.] Work the first 49 rows of the yoke pattern given for back.
To shape the neck: Continuing in yoke pattern, bind off 12 sts. at the beginning of the next row, then dec. 1 st. at the neck edge on the next 13 rows.
On 48 sts. work 3 rows.
To slope the shoulder: Continuing with m. in s.s., bind off 12 sts. at the beginning of the next row and the 2 following alternate rows. On 12 sts. work 1 row, then bind off.
Neckband: With right side of work facing rejoin m. and using size "B" needles pick up and k. 30 sts. from neck edge and work 7 rows in single rib. Bind off in rib.
Buttonband: With size "B" needles and m. cast on 8 sts. and work 190 rows in single rib, then bind off in rib.

Right Front

Work as given for left front until ★★ is reached.
Foundation row: With m. k.5, ★ p.6, k.6; repeat from ★ ending last repeat k.3. Now work the fish pattern as follows:
1st row: With m. p.1, k.4, (p.2, k.4) 4 times, s.s.k., with a. s.c., with m. k.2tog., k.1, p.2, k.1, with d. k.4, with m. p.1, (k.4, p.2) twice, k.4, p.1, with a. k.3, with m. k.2, p.2, k.2, with d. k.1, with m. k.1, p.2, k.1.
2nd row: With m. p.3, with a. p.2, with d. p.1, with m. k.4, with d. p.4, with m. p.3, k.6, p.6, k.3, p.1, with d. p.3, with m. p.5, with a. p.2, with m. p.1, with a. p.2, with m. k.3, (p.6, k.6) twice, p.3. The last 2 rows set the position of the pattern given in the chart. Work the 3rd to 81st rows from the chart.
82nd row: P.2tog., p.3, (k.6, p.6) 5 times, k.6, p.3. Mark the beginning of the last row with a colored thread to denote armhole. [73 sts.] Work the first 50 pattern rows of the yoke given for the back.
To shape the neck: Work as given for left front neck shaping to end.
Neckband: As given for left front.
Buttonhole band: With size "B" needles and m. cast on 8 sts. and work 4 rows in single rib.

1st Buttonhole row: Rib 3, bind off 2, rib to end.
2nd Buttonhole row: Rib 3, turn, cast on 2 over those bound off, turn, rib 3. Rib 28 rows.
Repeat the last 30 rows 5 times more, then work the 2 buttonhole rows again. Rib 4 rows. Bind off in rib.
Pocket backs (2 alike): With size "A" needles and m. cast on 30 sts. and work 40 rows in s.s., then bind off.

Sleeves
Both alike: Work as given for Sweater Pattern.

Making Up
Do not press. Sew bound off edges of sleeves to the straight row ends between the marking threads on back and fronts. Join sleeve and side seams, neatly sewing pocket backs in place in side seams and on wrong side of fronts, above the ribbing. Sew button- and buttonhole bands in place. Sew on buttons.

summer variations

Long Raj Sweater

LEFT
Elephant, umbrella and mosque motifs in a bold mix of colors set the exotic eastern tone of this design.
PATTERN PAGE 142

Patchwork Roses Vest

ABOVE RIGHT
A stylish hood distinguishes this floral vest. Knitted in fine cotton, it is light enough to wear on the beach.
PATTERN PAGE 122

Camels Jacket

BELOW RIGHT
Richly colored motifs, accentuated by waves of orient blue, make for a very striking version of the Camels design.
PATTERN PAGE 100

a u t u m n

After the bright sunshine and vibrant colors of summer, it can be quite a pleasant change when cooler weather returns and there is the opportunity to slip into cosy woollen knits. Autumnal colors may be more muted and subtle, but they are just as exciting. An additional element in this autumn collection is the delightful animal theme, with fun motifs of cats, bears and camels providing just the special touch needed to make a garment truly distinctive. The thick cotton used in the Alpine Sweater makes it ideal for an Indian summer, while other designs, knitted in wool, are warm enough for the coolest autumn days.

FROM LEFT TO RIGHT:
CATS SWEATER, BEARS SWEATER, CAMELS SWEATER
AND ALPINE SWEATER

c a t s

The cat motifs for these roomy, tuniclike sweaters are knitted separately then sewn onto the front or back.

A U T U M N

Child's Cats Sweater

PHOTOGRAPH THIS PAGE

Materials
For the sweater: 4 (7) (11) (15) 50 gram balls of "Patricia Roberts Pure Wool No.2" in main color. A pair each of size 6 and size 2 Aero knitting needles and a medium-size cable needle.
For the Cat in the Heart motif (optional): For the contrast colors, small amounts of each of the following: c., d. and e. in "Patricia Roberts Angora," f. in "Patricia Roberts Chenille," a. in "Patricia Roberts Extra Thick Wool" and b. and g. in "Patricia Roberts Pure Wool No.2." A pair of size 3 Aero knitting needles.
"Patricia Roberts Knitting Kits" containing sufficient yarn for the sweater and either part balls of the contrast colors, or the ready-knitted cat motif, are available from suppliers (see page 159).

Colors
m. = donkey brown
Contrasts for optional motif: a. = sand, b. = khaki, c. = white, d. = grey, e. = black, f. = pink, g. = olive.

Needle Sizes
Use size 6 needles for those referred to as size "A," size 2 needles for those referred to as size "B" and size 3 needles for those referred to as size "C" in the pattern.

A U T U M N

Woman's Cats Sweater

PHOTOGRAPH OVERLEAF

Materials
For the sweater: 17 50 gram balls of "Patricia Roberts

A U T U M N

Child's Cats Sweater
RIGHT

Woman's Cats Sweater
OVERLEAF

Pure Wool No.2" in main color. A pair each of size 6 and size 2 Aero knitting needles and a medium-size cable needle.

For the Two Cat motif (optional): For the contrast colors, small amounts of each of the following: a., b., c. and d. in "Patricia Roberts Angora," e. in "Patricia Roberts Chenille" and f. and g. in "Patricia Roberts Pure Wool No.2." A pair of size 3 Aero knitting needles.

Colors
Woman's sweater: m. = olive
Contrasts for optional motif: a. = black, b. = white, c. = sand, d. = brown, e. = pink, f. = khaki, g. = olive.

Needle Sizes
Use size 6 needles for those referred to as size "A," size 2 needles for those referred to as size "B" and size 3 needles for those referred to as size "C" in the pattern.

Abbreviations
cable 6, slip next 3 sts. onto cable needle at front of work, k.3, then k.3 from cable needle ■ **cr.3rt.**, cross 3 right thus, slip next st. onto cable needle at back of work, k.2, then k.1 from cable needle ■ **cr.3lt.**, cross 3 left thus, slip next 2 sts. onto cable needle at front of work, k.1, then k.2 from cable needle.

Tension
11 stitches and 16 rows to 2 in (5 cm) over the garter stitch stripe pattern and 13 stitches and 14 rows to 2 in (5 cm) over the cable pattern, each using size "A" needles.

Sweater Pattern

Measurements

	3-4 years	5-7 years	9-11 years
Underarms:	28 in (70 cm)	35 in (87.5 cm)	42 in (105 cm)
Side seam:	8¼ in (20 cm)	10¾ in (27 cm)	13¾ in (34 cm)
Length:	14 in (35 cm)	18¼ in (46 cm)	23 in (57.5 cm)
Sleeve seam:	8 in (20 cm)	12 in (30 cm)	15 in (37.5 cm)

	12-14 years	woman's
Underarms:	49 in (122.5 cm)	56 in (140 cm)
Side seam:	16¾ in (42 cm)	18¾ in (47 cm)
Length:	27¼ in (68 cm)	30½ in (76 cm)
Sleeve seam:	16 in (40 cm)	17 in (42.5 cm)

Back
With size "A" needles cast on 92 (114) (136) (158) (180) sts. and work in cable pattern as follows.

1st row: K.4, p.4, k.1, p.1, k.6, ★ p.1, k.1, p.1, k.1, p.2, k.4, p.2, k.1, p.1, k.1, p.1 ★★, k.6; repeat from ★ until 10 remain, p.1, k.1, p.1, k.3, p.3, k.1.

2nd row: K.4, p.3, k.1, p.1, k.1, p.6, ★ k.1, p.1, k.1, p.1, k.2, p.4, k.2, p.1, k.1, p.1, k.1 ★★, p.6; repeat from ★ until 10 remain, k.1, p.1, k.4, p.3, k.1.

3rd row: K.1, p.3, k.3, p.1, k.1, p.1, k.6, ★ p.1, k.1, p.1, k.1, p.1, cr.3rt., cr.3lt., p.1, k.1, p.1, k.1, p.1 ★★, k.6; repeat from ★ until 10 remain, p.1, k.1, p.4, k.4.

4th row: K.1, p.3, k.4, p.1, k.1, p.6, ★ k.1, p.1, k.1, p.1, k.1, p.2, k.1, p.3, k.1, p.1, k.1, p.1, k.1 ★★, p.6; repeat from ★ until 10 remain, k.1, p.1, k.1, p.3, k.4.

5th row: K.1, p.3, k.3, p.1, k.1, p.1, cable 6, ★ p.1, k.1, p.1, k.1, cr.3rt., p.1, k.1, cr.3lt., k.1, p.1, k.1, p.1 ★★, cable 6; repeat from ★ until 10 remain, p.1, k.1, p.4, k.4.

6th row: K.1, p.3, k.4, p.1, k.1, p.6, ★ k.1, p.1, k.1, p.4, k.1, p.1, k.1, p.3, k.1, p.1, k.1 ★★, p.6; repeat from ★ until 10 remain, k.1, p.1, k.1, p.3, k.4.

7th row: K.4, p.4, k.1, p.1, k.6; ★ p.1, k.1, p.1, cr.3rt., k.1, p.1, k.1, p.1, cr.3lt., p.1, k.1, p.1 ★★, k.6; repeat from ★ until 10 remain, p.1, k.1, p.1, k.3, p.3, k.1.

8th row: K.4, p.3, k.1, p.1, k.1, p.6, ★ k.1, p.1, k.1, p.2, k.1, p.1, k.1, p.1, k.1, p.3, k.1, p.1, k.1 ★★, p.6; repeat from ★ until 10 remain, k.1, p.1, k.4, p.3, k.1.

9th row: K.4, p.4, k.1, p.1, k.6, ★ p.1, k.1, p.1, k.2, p.1, k.1, p.1, k.1, p.1, k.3, p.1, k.1, p.1 ★★, k.6; repeat from ★ until 10 remain, p.1, k.1, p.1, k.3, p.3, k.1.

10th row: As 8th row.

11th row: K.1, p.3, k.3, p.1, k.1, p.1, k.6, ★ p.1, k.1, p.1, cr.3lt., k.1, p.1, k.1, p.1, p.1, cr.3rt., p.1, k.1, p.1 ★★, k.6; repeat from ★ until 10 remain, p.1, k.1, p.4, k.4.

12th row: As 6th row.

13th row: K.1, p.3, k.3, p.1, k.1, p.1, cable 6, ★ p.1, k.1, p.1, k.1, cr.3lt., p.1, k.1, cr.3rt., k.1, p.1, k.1, p.1 ★★, cable 6; repeat from ★ until 10 remain, p.1, k.1, p.4, k.4.

14th row: As 4th row.

15th row: K.4, p.4, k.1, p.1, k.6, ★ p.1, k.1, p.1, k.1, p.1, cr.3lt., cr.3rt., p.1, k.1, p.1, k.1, p.1 ★★, k.6; repeat from ★ until 10 remain, p.1, k.1, p.1, k.3, p.3, k.1.

16th row: As 2nd row.

The last 16 rows form the pattern. Repeat them 1 (1) (2) (2) (3) times more.

Decrease row: K. 1 (2) (3) (4) (5), ★ k.2tog., k.5; repeat from ★ to end. [79 (98) (117) (136) (155) sts.] With m. k. 1 row.

Now work in g.st. stripe pattern as follows:

1st row: All k.

2nd row: All p.

3rd and 4th rows: All k.

Repeat the last 4 rows 6 (11) (12) (18) (18) times more.

To shape the armholes: Bind off 6 sts. at the beginning of the next 2 rows.

On 67 (86) (105) (124) (143) sts. work 10 rows more in g.st. stripe pattern.

Increase row: K.5, ★ up 1, k.6; repeat from ★ ending last repeat k. 2 (3) (4) (5) (6). [78 (100) (122) (144) (166) sts.] Now work in cable pattern as follows:

Foundation row: With wrong side of work facing, k.1, p.1, k.1, p.6, work from ★ on 2nd cable-pattern row as given at beginning until 3 remain, k.1, p.1, k.1.

1st row: P.1, k.1, p.1, k.6, work from ★ on 1st cable-pattern row given at beginning, until 3 remain, p.1, k.1, p.1.

2nd row: K.1, p.1, k.1, p.6, work from ★ on 2nd cable-pattern row, until 3 remain, k.1, p.1, k.1.★★★

The last 2 rows set the position of the pattern given at the beginning. Continuing in cable pattern as set work 24 (36) (48) (58) (66) rows straight.

To slope the shoulders: Bind off 21 (29) (37) (45) (56) sts. at the beginning of the next 2 rows.

Bind off the remaining 36 (42) (48) (54) (54) sts.

Front

Work as given for back until ★★★ is reached.

Continuing in cable pattern as set, work 15 (25) (35) (45) (53) rows.

Now divide the sts. for the neck:

Next row: Pattern 28 (37) (46) (55) (66) and leave these sts. on a spare needle until required for right front shoulder, bind off 22 (26) (30) (34) (34) sts. for the neck, pattern to end and continue on these 28 (37) (46) (55) (66) sts. for the left front shoulder.

Left front shoulder: To shape the neck: Dec. 1 st. at the neck edge on each of the next 7 (8) (9) (10) (10) rows.

On 21 (29) (37) (45) (56) sts. work 1 (2) (3) (2) (2) rows.

To slope the shoulder: Bind off.

Right front shoulder: With right side of work facing rejoin yarn to inner edge of sts. left on spare needle and work to end of row, then work as given for left front shoulder to end.

Sleeves

Both alike: With size "B" needles cast on 40 (46) (52) (58) (62) sts. and k. 4 rows, then work 8 (12) (16) (24) (24) rows in double rib.

Change to size "A" needles and work in g.st. stripe pattern with center cable panel as follows:

1st row: K. 12 (15) (18) (21) (23), work from ★ to ★★ on first cable pattern row given for back, k. 12 (15) (18) (21) (23).

2nd row: K. 12 (15) (18) (21) (23), work from ★ to ★★ on 2nd cable row given for back, k. to end.

3rd row: K. 12 (15) (18) (21) (23), work from ★ to ★★ on 3rd cable row, k. to end.

4th row: P. 12 (15) (18) (21) (23), work from ★ to ★★ on 4th cable row, p. to end.

Continuing to work in this 4-row pattern, with center panel in cable pattern as given between ★ and ★★ on the 16 cable-pattern rows given for back, inc. 1 st. at each end of the next row and then every 4th (6th) (6th) (6th) (6th) row 10 (12) (15) (15) (17) times.

On 62 (72) (84) (90) (98) sts. pattern 9 (5) (7) (7) (3) rows. Mark each end of the last row with colored threads.

Pattern 8 rows more.

Bind off 23 (28) (34) (37) (41) sts. at the beginning of the next 2 rows.

Change to size "B" needles and on 16 sts. work 20 (28) (36) (44) (56) rows in cable pattern, then bind off.

Neckband

First set in right sleeve, so that the sts. bound off at underarms are sewn to the row ends above the marking threads on the sleeve and so that the cable panel at top of sleeve is sewn to the shoulders with the 16 st. bound off group forming part of neck edge. In the same way sew the left sleeve to the front only.

Now with right side of work facing, rejoin yarn to the 16 st. cable panel at top of left sleeve and using size "B" needles, pick up and k. 22 (24) (26) (26) (26) sts. from cable panel and left front neck edge, 18 (22) (26) (28) (28) sts. from center front, 22 (24) (26) (26) (26) sts. from right front neck edge and top of cable panel and 30 (36) (40) (46) (46) sts. from back neck edge. On 92 (106) (118) (126) (126) sts. work 9 (11) (13) (15) (15) rows in double rib, then k. 4 rows and p. 1 row, and bind off loosely.

Making Up

Set in left back sleeve and join shoulder seam, continuing seam across neckband. Join sleeve seams. Join side seams, beginning half way up the cable pattern at lower edge. Do not press.

Cats Motifs

Abbreviations

m.k., make knot thus, on right side rows, with a. k.1, sl. the st. just made onto left-hand needle and p. the st. just made; on wrong side rows, read p. for k. and k. for p. ■ **3 from 1**, k. into front, back and front again of the same st.

Tension

12 stitches and 20 rows to 2 in (5 cm) over the moss stitch using size "C" needles.

Cat in Heart Motif

With size "C" needles and m. cast on 3 sts. and work as follows:

1st row: With m. p.3.

2nd row: With m. p.1, 3 from 1, p.1.

3rd row: With m. p.5.

4th row: With m. p.1, 3 from 1, p.1, 3 from 1, p.1.

5th row: With m. p.2, k.2, with a, m.k., with m. k.2, p.2.

6th row: With m. p.1, 3 from 1, p.1, with a. m.k., with b. p.1, with a. m.k., with m. p.1, 3 from 1, p.1.

Work the 7th to 49th rows from the chart.

Now divide the sts.:

50th row: Pattern from chart up to center st. and leave these 12 sts. until required, bind off center st., pattern to end and continue on these 12 sts.

Work the 51st to 53rd rows from the chart, then bind off the remaining 8 sts.

With right side of work facing, rejoin yarn to the 12 sts. left on needle and work the 51st to 53rd rows from the chart, then bind off the remaining 8 sts.

Two Cat Motif

With size "C" needles and m. cast on 60 sts. and k. 4 rows.

Using separate small balls of color for each section of the pattern and taking care not to pull colors not in use tightly across the back of the work, work the 5th to 46th rows from the chart, then bind off.

Completion

Neatly sew either motif on the back or front of the sweater as desired.

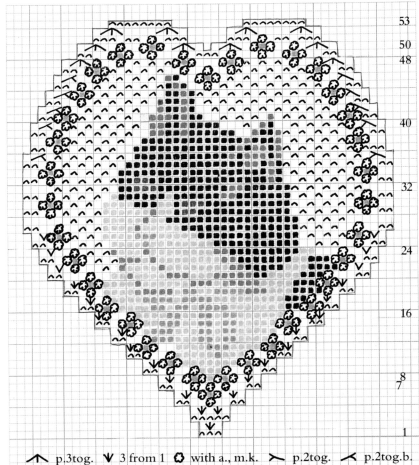

⋏ p.3tog. ⋎ 3 from 1 ✿ with a., m.k. ⟩ p.2tog. ⟨ p.2tog.b.
⋎ inc. ⌃ with m., k. on w.s., p. on r.s. ☐ with m., k. on r.s., p. on w.s.
▪ b. ▪ c. ▪ d. ▪ e. ▪ f. ▪ g.

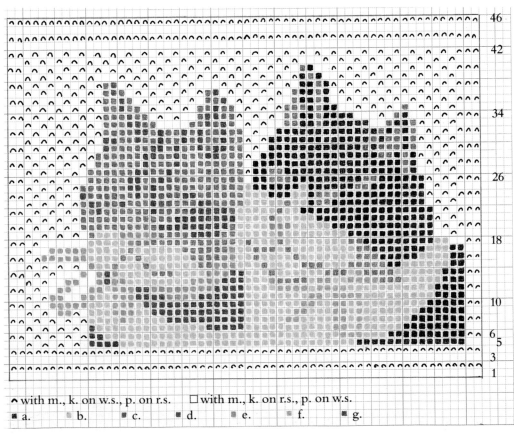

⌃ with m., k. on w.s., p. on r.s. ☐ with m., k. on r.s., p. on w.s.
▪ a. ▪ b. ▪ c. ▪ d. ▪ e. ▪ f. ▪ g.

b e a r s

Mischievous-looking bears in varying guises pad over these roll-neck sweaters.

AUTUMN

Thin Bears Sweater
PHOTOGRAPH THIS PAGE

Materials
24 25 gram balls of "Patricia Roberts Pure Wool No.1" in main color, and 3 balls of the same yarn in contrast d. and 1 ball in contrast c.; plus 2 25 gram balls of "Patricia Roberts Angora" in contrast a. and 1 ball in b. A pair each of size 5 and size 3 Aero knitting needles and a fine cable needle.

Colors
m. = khaki, a. = sand, b. = brown angora, c. = black, d. = brown wool.

Needle Sizes
Use size 5 needles for those referred to as size "A" and size 3 needles for those referred to as size "B" in the pattern.

AUTUMN

Thick Bears Sweater
PHOTOGRAPH THIS PAGE

Materials
19 50 gram balls of "Patricia Roberts Pure Wool No.2" in main color, and 1 ball of the same yarn in contrast c.; plus 1 25 gram ball of "Patricia Roberts Angora" in each of the contrasts a. and b. A pair each of size 6 and size 3 Aero knitting needles and a medium-size cable needle.

Colors
m. and d. = brown wool, a. = sand, b. = brown angora, c. = black.

Needle Sizes
Use size 6 needles for those referred to as size "A" and size 3 needles for those referred to as size "B" in the pattern.

AUTUMN

Thin Bears Sweater
CENTER RIGHT
AND OPPOSITE

Thick Bears Sweater
ABOVE RIGHT (*right*)
AND BELOW
RIGHT (*left*)

WINTER

Thin Bears Sweater
PAGE 137

WINTER

Thin Bears Sweater

PHOTOGRAPH PAGE 137

Materials

25 25 gram balls of "Patricia Roberts Pure Wool No.1" in main color, and 1 ball of the same yarn in contrast c.; plus 2 25 gram balls of "Patricia Roberts Angora" in contrast a. and 1 ball in contrast b. A pair each of size 5 and size 3 Aero knitting needles and a fine cable needle.

Colors

m. and d. = white wool, a. = white angora, b. = sand, c. = black.

Needle Sizes

Use size 5 needles for those referred to as size "A" and size 3 needles for those referred to as size "B" in the pattern.

Abbreviations

cable 4, k.2, slip next 2 sts. onto a cable needle at front of work, k.2, then k.2 from cable needle ■ **cable 10**, slip next 5 sts. onto a cable needle and leave at front of work, k.5, then k.5 from cable needle.

Sweater Pattern

Thin Bears Sweater

Tension

16 stitches and 20 rows to 2 in (5 cm) over the pattern using size "A" needles.

Measurements

Underarms: 42½ in (106 cm). Side seam: 20 in (50 cm). Length: 29½ in (74 cm). Sleeve seam: 17 in (42.5 cm).

Thick Bears Sweater

Tension

14 stitches and 18 rows to 2 in (5 cm) over the pattern using size "A" needles.

Measurements

Underarms: 49 in (123 cm). Side seam: 19 in (47.5 cm). Length: 29½ in (74 cm). Sleeve seam: 17½ in (44 cm).

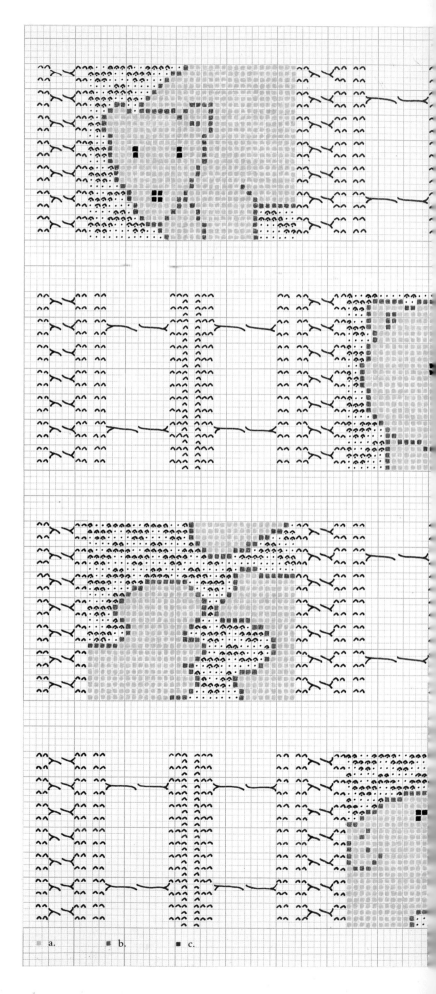

a.   ■ b.   ■ c.

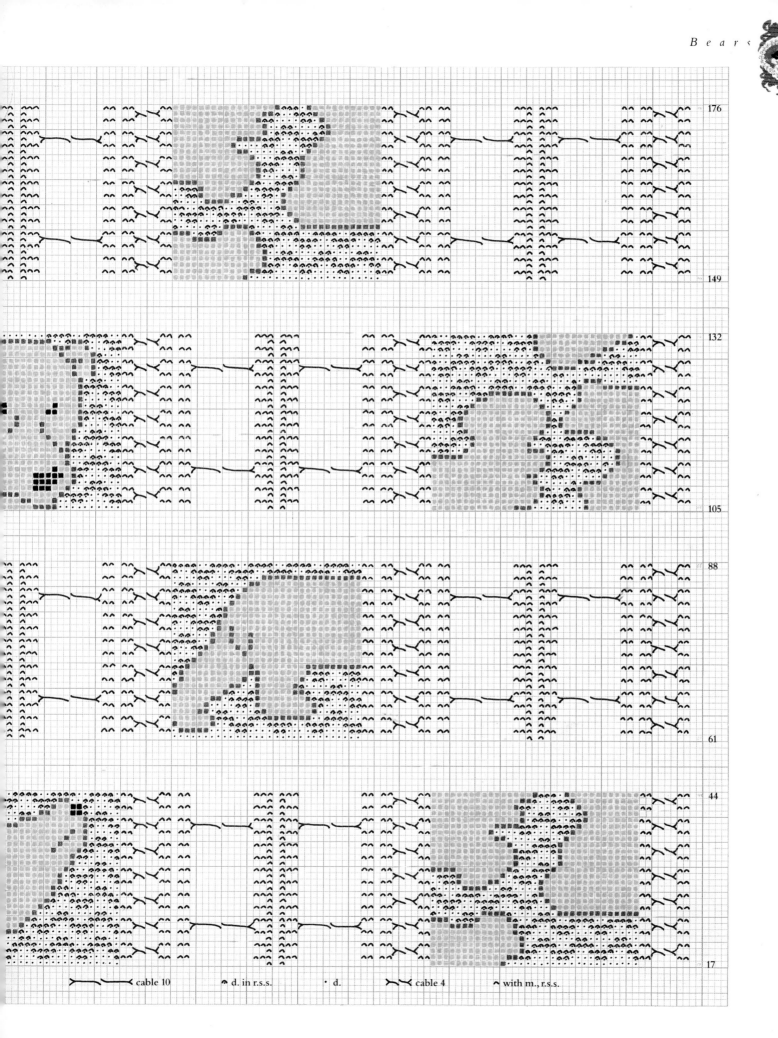

176

149

132

105

88

61

44

17

⟩—⟨ cable 10   ⌒ d. in r.s.s.   · d.   ⟩—⟨ cable 4   ⌒ with m., r.s.s.

Back

With size "B" needles and m. cast on 172 sts. and work in pattern as follows:

1st to 4th rows: With m. all k.

5th row: K.10, ★ p.1, k.1, p.1, k.2, p.1, k.4, p.1, k.2, p.1, k.1, p.1, k.2, p.1, k.4, p.1, k.2, p.1, k.1, p.1, k.12; repeat from ★ ending last repeat k.10.

6th row: With m. k.2, p.4, k.2, ★ p.2, k.1, p.1, k.1, p.2, k.1, p.4, k.1, p.2, k.1, p.1, k.1, p.2, k.1, p.4, k.1, p.2, k.1, p.1, k.1, p.2, k.2, p.4, k.2; repeat from ★ to end.

7th row: With m. k.2, cable 4, k.2, ★ p.3, k.1, p.4, cable 4, p.4, k.1, p.4, cable 4, p.4, k.1, p.3, k.2, cable 4, k.2; repeat from ★ to end.

8th row: With m. k.2, p.4, k.5, ★ p.1, k.4, p.4, k.4, p.1, k.4, p.4, k.4, p.1, k.5, p.4, k.5; repeat from ★ ending last repeat k.2.

Repeat the 5th to 8th rows 3 times more for the Thin Sweater or 6 times more for the Thick Sweater.

Change to size "A" needles and work in main pattern as follows: Use separate balls of contrast color for each section of the pattern and separate balls of m. at each side of color motifs.

1st to 8th rows: As 1st to 8th rows given before.

9th to 12th rows: As 5th to 8th rows.

13th to 16th rows: With m. all k.

For the Thin Bears Sweater:

17th to 44th rows: Work in pattern from chart.

45th to 60th rows: With m. as given for 1st to 16th rows.

For the Thick Bears Sweater:

The 17th to 60th rows are omitted.

For both the Thin and Thick Bears Sweaters:

61st to 88th rows: Work in pattern from chart.

89th to 104th rows: As given for 1st to 16th rows.

105th to 132nd rows: As given in chart.

133rd to 148th rows: As for 1st to 16th rows.

149th to 176th rows: As given in chart.

Now work the 1st to 6th pattern rows again.

To shape the armholes: Continuing in pattern, bind off 8 sts. at the beginning of the next 2 rows.

On 156 sts. work the 9th to 16th rows.

Now work in yoke pattern as follows:

1st row: K.15, ★ p.1, k.1, p.1, k.38; repeat from ★ ending last repeat k.15.

2nd row: ★★ P.1, k.2, p.10, k.3, p.1, k.3, p.10, k.2, p.1 ★, k.2, p.4, k.2; repeat from ★★ but ending last repeat at ★.

3rd row: K.15, ★ p.1, k.1, p.1, k.17, cable 4, k.17; repeat from ★ until 18 remain, p.1, k.1, p.1, k.15.

4th row: As 2nd row.

5th and 6th rows: As 1st and 2nd rows.

7th row: K.3, cable 10, k.2, p.1, k.1, p.1, k.2, cable 10,
★ k.5, cable 4, k.5, cable 10, k.2, p.1, k.1, p.1, k.2,
cable 10; repeat from ★ until 3 remain k.3.
8th row: As 2nd row.
9th to 20th rows: Repeat 1st to 4th rows, 3 times.
21st and 22nd rows: As 1st and 2nd rows.
23rd row: As 7th row.
24th row: As 2nd row.
25th to 28th rows: As 1st to 4th rows.
The last 28 rows form the cable pattern.★★★
Repeat them once more, then work the first 24 rows
again.
To slope the shoulders: Bind off 10 sts. at the
beginning of the next 10 rows.
Bind off the remaining 56 sts.

Front

Work as given for back until ★★★ is reached.
Repeat the last 28 rows once more, then work the first
row again.
Now divide the sts. for the neck:
Next row: Pattern 64 and leave these sts. on a spare
needle until required for right front shoulder, bind off
28 for the neck, pattern to end and continue on these
64 sts. for the left front shoulder.
Left front shoulder: To shape the neck: Dec. 1 st. at
the neck edge on each of the next 14 rows.
On 50 sts. work 8 rows.
To slope the shoulder: Bind off 10 sts. at the
beginning of the next row and the 3 following alternate
rows. On 10 sts. work 1 row, then bind off.
Right front shoulder: With right side of work facing
rejoin yarn to inner edge of sts. left on spare needle
and pattern to end of row, then work as given for left
front shoulder to end.

Collar

For the Thin Bears Sweater:
With size "B" needles and m. cast on 204 sts. and k. 5
rows.
Next row: K.4, ★ k.2tog., k.3; repeat from ★ to end.
[164 sts.]
Work 40 rows in double rib, then bind off loosely in
rib.
For the Thick Bears Sweater:
With size "B" needles and m. cast on 164 sts. and
work 60 rows in double rib, then bind off loosely in
rib.

Sleeves

Both alike: With size "B" needles and m. cast on 64
sts. and k. 5 rows, then work 23 rows in double rib.

Increase row: Rib 5, ★ up 1, rib 6; repeat from ★ ending
last repeat rib 5. [74 sts.]
Change to size "A" needles and work the first 10 rows
of pattern given for yoke.
Continuing in yoke pattern as set and working the
extra sts. in garter st. as they occur, inc. 1 st. at
each end of the next row and then every 4th row 29
times.
On 134 sts. pattern 15 rows for the Thin Sweater or 3
rows for the Thick Sweater. Mark each end of the last
row with colored threads.
Pattern 10 rows straight, then bind off loosely.

Making Up

Do not press. Join shoulder seams. Join row end edges
of collar. Neatly sew bound off edge of collar in place
all round neck edge. Set in sleeves, so that the row
ends above the marking threads are sewn to the sts.
bound off at underarms. Join sleeve and side seams.

autumn variations

Bobbles Jacket

LEFT
Knitted in Extra Thick Wool, this version of the Bobbles design is warm enough to take the place of a coat.
PATTERN PAGE 70

Lilacs Sweater

ABOVE RIGHT
The black background of this chunky wool sweater offsets dramatic lilac-blossom motifs in red, pink, plum, khaki and olive.
PATTERN PAGE 64

Short Paisley Sweater

BELOW RIGHT
A cropped version of the Paisley design rings the changes in autumnal olive green.
PATTERN PAGE 50

c a m e l s

Knitted in wool for autumn or cotton for spring and summer, this rich design is based on a desert theme.

A U T U M N

Camels Sweater

PHOTOGRAPH THIS PAGE

Materials
18 25 gram balls of "Patricia Roberts Pure Wool No.1" in main color, 3 balls of the same yarn in each of the contrasts a. and e., 2 balls in each of the contrasts b., d. and h. and 1 ball in each of the contrasts c. and g.; plus 2 balls of "Patricia Roberts Angora" in contrast f. and a small amount in contrast i. A pair each of size 3 and size 2 Aero knitting needles and a fine cable needle.

Colors
m. = airforce blue, a. = royal blue, b. = sap green, c. = khaki, d. = brown, e. = faded violet, f. = sand, g. = purple, h. = olive, i. = dark gray.

Needle Sizes
Use size 3 needles for those referred to as size "A" and size 2 needles for those referred to as size "B" in the pattern.

A U T U M N

Camels Jacket

PHOTOGRAPH THIS PAGE

Materials
11 50 gram balls of "Patricia Roberts Pure Wool No.2" in main color, 3 balls of the same yarn in contrast e. and 1 ball in each of the contrasts b., c. and h.; plus 1 100 gram ball of "Patricia Roberts Extra Thick Wool" in each of the contrasts a., d. and f. A pair each of size 3 and size 6 Aero knitting needles, and a medium-size cable needle and 10 buttons.

Colors
m. = faded violet, a. = royal blue, b. = donkey brown, c. and g. = khaki, d. = plum, e. = airforce blue, f. = sand, h. and i. = olive.

AUTUMN

Camels Sweater
ABOVE RIGHT, BELOW RIGHT AND OPPOSITE

Camels Jacket
CENTER RIGHT

SPRING

Camels Sweater
PAGE 28

SUMMER

Camels Jacket
PAGE 83

Needle Sizes

Use size 6 needles for those referred to as size "A" and size 3 needles for those referred to as size "B" in the pattern.

SPRING

Camels Sweater

PHOTOGRAPH PAGE 28

Materials

11 25 gram balls of "Patricia Roberts Extra Fine Cotton" in main color white and for the contrast colors in 25 gram balls of "Patricia Roberts Fine Cotton": 5 balls of sand and 2 balls each of taupe, mustard and coral. A pair each of size 2 and size 1 Aero knitting needles and a fine cable needle.

Colors

On Chart A: m. = white, a. = sand, b. = sand, c. = mustard, d. = coral.

On Chart B: m. = white, a. = taupe, b. = white, c. = mustard, d. = coral, e. = sand, f. = taupe, g. = sand, h. = white, i. = sand.

On Chart C: b. = white, c. = mustard, e. = sand, g. = taupe.

Needle Sizes

Use size 2 needles for those referred to as size "A" and size 1 needles for those referred to as size "B" in the pattern.

SUMMER

Camels Jacket

PHOTOGRAPH PAGE 83

Materials

11 50 gram balls of "Patricia Roberts Cotton No.2" in main color and 2 balls of the same yarn in contrast a., 3 balls in contrast e. and 1 ball in each of the contrasts b., c., d., g. and h.; plus 2 50 gram balls of "Patricia Roberts Extra Thick Cotton" in f. A pair each of size 3 and size 5 Aero knitting needles, a medium-size cable needle and 10 buttons.

Colors

m. = mauve, a. = orient blue, b. = coral, c. = fuchsia, d. = red, e. = navy, f. = sand, g. = mustard, h. and i. = khaki.

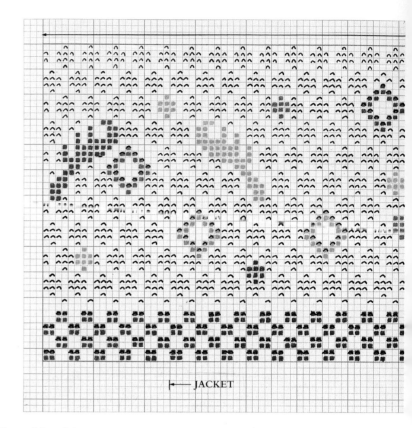

←— JACKET

Needle Sizes

Use size 5 needles for those referred to as size "A" and size 3 needles for those referred to as size "B" in the pattern.

Abbreviations

cr.3, cross 3 thus, slip next 2 sts. onto cable needle at front of work, with background color k.1, with d. k.2 from cable needle ■ **c.4f.**, cable 4 front thus, slip next 2 sts. onto cable needle at front of work, k.2, then k.2 from cable needle ■ **m.b.**, make bobble thus, with appropriate color k.1, y.r.n., k.1 all into one st., turn, p.3, turn, k.3, turn, p.3, turn, with background color sl.1, k.2tog., p.s.s.o. ■ **m.k.**, make knot thus, with g. p. into back and front of st., turn, k.2, turn, with background color, p.2tog.

Sweater Pattern

Autumn Camels Sweater

Tension

14 stitches and 18 rows to 2 in (5 cm) over the background pattern using size "A" needles.

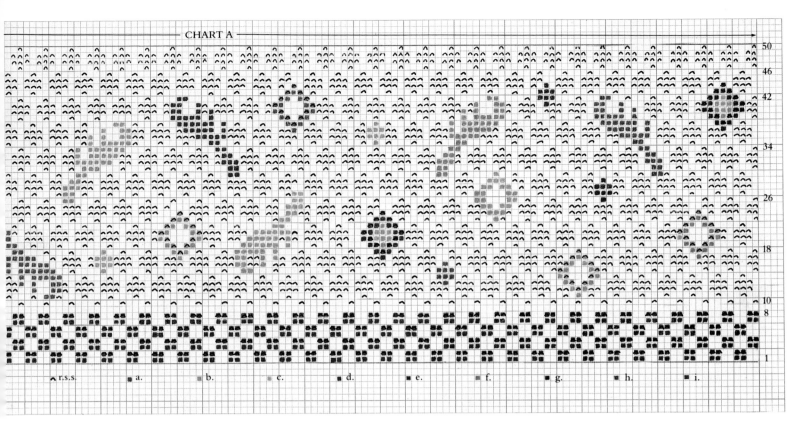

CHART A

➔ r.s.s.　■ a.　■ b.　■ c.　■ d.　■ e.　■ f.　■ g.　■ h.　■ i.

M e a s u r e m e n t s
Underarms: 50 in (125 cm). Side seam: 18½ in (46 cm).
Length: 28 in (70 cm). Sleeve seam: 17 in (42.5 cm).

Spring Camels Sweater

T e n s i o n
16 stitches and 20 rows to 2 in (5 cm) over the
background pattern using size "A" needles.

M e a s u r e m e n t s
Underarms: 44 in (110 cm). Side seam: 16½ in (41 cm).
Length: 25½ in (63 cm). Sleeve seam: 17 in (42.5 cm).

B a c k
With size "B" needles and e. cast on 176 sts. by the
thumb method. Break off e., join in m. and k.1 row,
then work 19 rows in double rib.
Change to size "A" needles and work in pattern from
the charts as follows. Use separate small balls of color
for each of the motifs, so that colors not in use are not
taken across the back of the work.
Working from Chart A:
1st row: ★ With m. k.2, with a. k.2; repeat from ★ to
end.

2nd row: ★ With a. k.2, with m. p.2; repeat from ★ to
end.
The last 2 rows set the position of the pattern given in
Chart A. Work the 3rd to 46th rows from the chart.
Now work the shell pattern as follows:
1st row: With m. k.9, turn, sl.1, p.8, turn, k.7, turn,
sl.1, p.6, turn, k.5, turn, sl.1, p.4, turn, k.3, turn,
sl.1, p.2, turn, k.31, ★ turn, sl.1, p.16, turn, sl.1, k.14,
turn, sl.1, p.12, turn, sl.1, k.10, turn, sl.1, p.8, turn,
sl.1, k.6, turn, sl.1, p.4 ★★, turn, k.33 ★; repeat from
★ to ★, ending last repeat k.24, turn, p.8, turn, sl.1,
k.7, turn, p.6, turn, sl.1, k.5, turn, p.4, turn, sl.1, k.3,
turn, p.2, turn, sl.1, k.1.
2nd row: With m. all k.
3rd and 4th rows: With e. all k.
5th row: With e. k.2, ★ y.r.n., sl.1, k.1, p.s.s.o.; repeat
from ★ to end.
6th row: With e. all k.
7th row: With e. k.13, ★ turn, (p.1, k.1) twice, sl.1,
turn, (p.1, k.1) 3 times, sl.1, turn, (p.1, k.1) 4 times,
sl.1, turn, (k.1, p.1) 5 times, sl.1, turn, (p.1, k.1) 6
times, sl.1, turn, (k.1, p.1) 7 times, sl.1, turn, (p.1,
k.1) 8 times, sl.1, turn, k.33; repeat from ★ ending last
repeat k.20.
8th row: With e. all k.
Break off e.

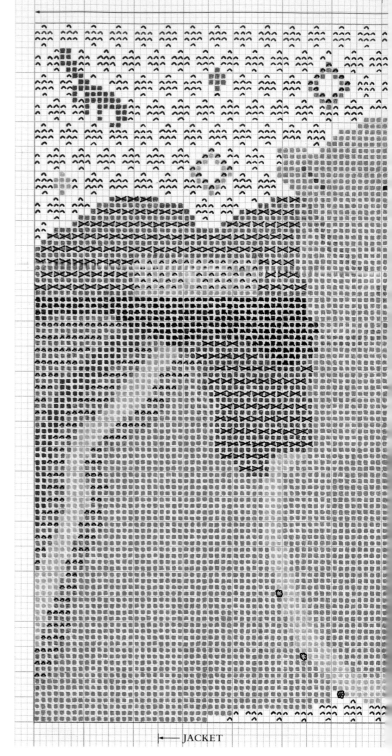

←— JACKET

Noting the information given at the beginning of the
pattern regarding color work, work the 1st to 108th
rows from Chart B, marking each end of the 92nd row
with colored threads to denote armholes. ★★★ Return
to Chart A and work the 11th to 46th rows, increasing
1 st. at the end of the last row.
Now work from Chart C as follows:
1st row: With m. work 8 sts. in background pattern as
before, ★ with e. k.1, with m. pattern 31; repeat from
★ ending last repeat with m. pattern 8.

112

104

96

88

80

72

64

56

48

40

32

24

16

8

1

✕ 2 from 2   ✕✕ c.4f.   ✕✕ with d., cr.3   ⌃ r.s.s.   ◆ m.k.   ✿ m.b.   ■ a.   ■ b.   ■ c.   ■ d.   ■ e.   ■ f.   ■ g.   ■ h.   ■ i.

2nd row: With m. pattern 7, ★ with e. p.3, with m. pattern 29; repeat from ★ ending last repeat, with m. pattern 7.

The last 2 rows set the position of the pattern given in Chart C. Work the 3rd to 18th rows from the chart. With e. k. 4 rows. With m. k. 1 row, then p. 1 row. Work the first 4 rows from Chart A.

To slope the shoulders: Continuing in pattern as set, bind off 20 sts. at the beginning of the next 6 rows. Bind off the remaining 57 sts. loosely.

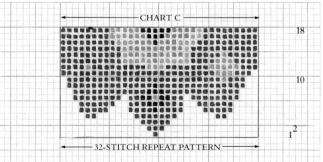

CHART C

18

10

2
1

◄— 32-STITCH REPEAT PATTERN —►

Front

Work as given for back until ★★★ is reached. Work the 11th to 37th rows from Chart A.

Now divide the sts. for the neck: Pattern 80 and leave these sts. on a spare needle until required for right front shoulder, bind off 16, pattern to end and continue on these 80 sts. for the left front shoulder.

Left front shoulder: To shape the neck: Continuing in pattern from Chart A, dec. 1 st. at the neck edge on each of the next 8 rows.

Now work from Chart C as follows:

1st row: With m. work 8 sts. in background pattern as before, ★ with e. k.1, with m. pattern 31; repeat from ★ to end.

The last row sets the position of the pattern given in Chart C. ★★ Dec. 1 st. at the neck edge on each of the next 12 rows. On 60 sts. work 5 rows, completing the pattern from Chart C.

With e. k. 4 rows. With m. k. 1 row and p. 1 row. With m. and a. work the first 4 rows from Chart A. (Work 1 extra row here, when working right front shoulder.)

To slope the shoulder: Continuing in pattern, bind off 20 sts. at the beginning of the next row and the following alternate row. On 20 sts. work 1 row, then bind off.

Right front shoulder: With right side of work facing, rejoin yarn to the inner edge of the sts. left on spare needle and pattern 8 rows, decreasing 1 st. at the neck edge on each row.

Now work from Chart C as follows:

1st row: ★ With m. work 31 sts. in background pattern as before, with e. k.1; repeat from ★ until 8 sts. remain, with m. pattern to end.

Work as for left front shoulder from ★★ to end, noting the variation in the rows.

Collar: With size "B" needles and m. cast on 138 sts. and work in rib as follows:

1st row: K.1, p.1, ★ k.2, p.2; repeat from ★ ending last repeat p.1, k.1.

2nd row: K.2, ★ p.2, k.2; repeat from ★ to end.

Repeat these 2 rows 15 times more.

Beginning with a k. row, s.s. 5 rows, then bind off.

Sleeves

Both alike: With size "B" needles and e. cast on 64 sts. and work 27 rows in double rib.

Increase row: Rib 2, ★ up 1, rib 4; repeat from ★ ending last repeat rib 2. [80 sts.]

Change to size "A" needles and work in pattern from Chart A as follows, noting the information regarding color work given for the back.

1st row: ★ With m. k.2, with a. k.2; repeat from ★ to end.

2nd row: ★ With a. k.2, with m. p.2; repeat from ★ to end.

3rd row: ★ With a. k.2, with m. k.2, repeat from ★ to end.

4th row: ★ With m. p.2, with a. k.2; repeat from ★ to end.

5th to 8th rows: As 1st to 4th rows.

9th row: With m. all k.

10th row: ★ With m. p.3, k.1; repeat from ★ to end.

11th row: With m. k.2, p.1, (k.3, p.1) 15 times, with d. k.2, with m. k.1, p.1, (k.3, p.1) 3 times, k.1.

The last 11 rows set the position of the pattern given in the center of Chart A. Now work the 12th row. The 11th to 50th rows of Chart A form the repeat pattern for the rest of the sleeves.

Continuing in pattern from chart and working the extra sts. in m. as they occur, inc. 1 st. at each end of the next row and then every 6th row 18 times.

On 118 sts. pattern 5 rows for the Autumn Sweater or 21 rows for the Spring Sweater.

To shape the sleeve top: Bind off 6 sts. at the beginning of the next 8 rows and 10 sts. on the 6 following rows. Then bind off the remaining 10 sts.

Making Up

Do not press. Join shoulder seams. Set in sleeves between the marking threads on back and front. Join sleeve and side seams. Neatly join the row ends of collar. With this seam to center front, neatly sew collar in place all round neck edge.

Jacket Pattern

Tension

12 stitches and 16 rows to 2 in (5 cm) over the background pattern, using size "A" needles.

Measurements

Underarms: 52 in (130 cm). Side seam: 18¼ in (46 cm). Length: 27¼ in (67 cm). Sleeve seam: 17½ in (44 cm).

Back

With size "B" needles and e. cast on 156 sts., by the thumb method, and work as given for back of sweater until 45 rows have been worked from Chart A, noting that the 20 sts. on the left-hand side of the chart are omitted for the jacket.

Work the 46th row from the chart, decreasing 1 st. at each end of the row. [154 sts.]

Work the 8-row shell pattern given for back of sweater, increasing 1 st. at each end of the last row. [156 sts.]

Work the 1st to 64th rows from Chart B, noting that the 20 sts. on the left-hand side of the chart are omitted for the jacket. Mark each end of the last row with colored threads to denote armholes.

Now work the 65th to 112th rows from Chart B, increasing 1 st. at the end of the last row. [157 sts.]

Now work from Chart C as follows:

1st row: With m. work 14 sts. in background pattern, ★ with e. k.1, with m. pattern 31; repeat from ★ ending last repeat pattern 14.

2nd row: With m. pattern 13, ★ with e. p.3, with m. pattern 29; repeat from ★ ending last repeat with m. pattern 13.

The last 2 rows set the position of the repeat pattern given in Chart C. Work the 3rd to 18th rows from the chart, decreasing 1 st. at the end of the last row. [156 sts.] With d. k. 2 rows.

To slope the shoulders: Working in s.s. with m., bind off 29 sts. at the beginning of the next 4 rows. Bind off the remaining 40 sts.

Left Front

With size "B" needles and e. cast on 78 sts. by the thumb method. Break off e., join in m. and k. 1 row, then work 19 rows in double rib.

Change to size "A" needles and work as follows from the right-hand side of Chart A. ★★

1st row: With m. k.2, ★ with a. k.2, with m. k.2; repeat from ★ to end.

2nd row: With m. p.2, ★ with a. k.2, with m. p.2; repeat from ★ to end.

3rd row: With a, k.2, ★ with m. k.2, with a. k.2; repeat from ★ to end.

Work the 4th to 9th rows from Chart A as set.

10th row: With m. p.1, k.1, ★ p.3, k.1; repeat from ★ to end.

11th row: With m. k.2, (p.1, k.3) 6 times, p.1, k.1, with b. k.1, with m. k.1, (p.1, k.3) 12 times.

Work the 12th to 46th rows from the right-hand side of Chart A. Now work in shell pattern as follows:

1st row: Work as given for 1st row of shell pattern on back of sweater, but ending last repeat turn, k.14.

2nd to 6th rows: As for back.

7th row: As for 7th row on back, but ending last repeat k.32, then turn, k.1, p.1, k.1, sl.1, turn, rib 4, turn, rib 5, sl.1, turn, rib 6, turn, rib 7, sl.1, turn, rib 8, turn, rib 9, sl.1, turn, rib 10.

8th row: With e. all k. Break off e.

Now work the 1st to 112th rows from Chart B,

marking the end of the 64th row with a colored thread to denote armhole.

Now work from Chart C as follows:

1st row: With m. work 14 sts. in background pattern, ★ with e. k.1, with m. pattern 31; repeat from ★ to end. The last row sets the position of the pattern.

To shape the neck: Continuing in pattern, bind off 10 sts. at the beginning of the next row, then dec. 1 st. at

the neck edge on each of the next 10 rows.
On 58 sts. pattern 6 rows.
With d. k. 2 rows.
To slope the shoulder: Bind off 29 sts. at the beginning of the next row. On 29 sts. work 1 row, then bind off.

Right Front

Work as given for left front until ** is reached.
1st row: With a. k.2, ★ with m. k.2, with a. k.2; repeat from ★ to end.
2nd row: With a. k.2, ★ with m. k.2, with a. k.2; repeat from ★ to end.
3rd to 9th rows: Work from Chart A as set.
10th row: ★ With m. k.3, p.1; repeat from ★ until 2 remain, k.2.
11th row: With m. p.1, (k.3, p.1) 8 times, with d. k.2, with m. k.1, (p.1, k.3) 10 times, p.1, k.1.
12th to 46th rows: Work in pattern from Chart A as set.
Now work in shell pattern as follows:
1st row: With m. k.21, then work from ★ on 1st row of shell pattern on back of sweater.
2nd to 6th rows: As 2nd to 6th rows on back.
7th row: With e. k.3, turn, p.1, k.1, p.1, turn, rib 4, sl.1, turn, rib 5, turn, rib 6, sl.1, turn, rib 7, turn, rib 8, sl.1, turn, rib 9, turn, k.33; work from ★ on 7th shell row on back to end.
8th row: With e. all k. Break off e.
Now work the 1st to 116th rows from Chart B, marking the beginning of the 64th row with a colored thread to denote armhole.
Now work from Chart C as follows:
1st row: ★ With m. work 31 sts. in background pattern, with e. k.1; repeat from ★ once, with m. pattern 14.
2nd row: With m. pattern 13, (with e. p.3, with m. pattern 29) twice, with e. p.1.
To shape the neck: Continuing in pattern, bind off 10 sts. at the beginning of the next row, then dec. 1 st. at the neck edge on each of the next 10 rows.
On 58 sts. pattern 5 rows.
With d. k. 2 rows.
Continuing with m. s.s., work 1 row.
To slope the shoulder: Bind off 29 sts. at the beginning of the next row. On 29 sts. work 1 row, then bind off.
Neckband: First join shoulder seams. With right side of work facing, rejoin m. to right front neck edge and using size "B" needles, pick up and k. 28 sts. from right front neck edge, 40 sts. from back neck edge and 28 sts. from left front neck edge.
On 96 sts. work 7 rows in double rib, then bind off in rib.

Buttonband: With size "B" needles and m. cast on 12 sts. and work 172 rows in double rib, then bind off in rib.
Buttonhole band: With size "B" needles and m. cast on 12 sts. and work 4 rows in double rib.
1st Buttonhole row: Rib 5, bind off 2, rib to end.
2nd Buttonhole row: Rib 5, turn, cast on 2, turn, rib to end.
Rib 16 rows.
Repeat the last 18 rows 8 times, then work the 2 buttonhole rows again.
Rib 4 rows, then bind off in rib.
Pocket backs (2 alike): With size "A" needles and m. cast on 30 sts. and s.s. 40 rows, then bind off.

Sleeves

Both alike: With size "B" needles and e. cast on 52 sts. and work 23 rows in single rib.
Increase row: Rib 4, ★ up 1, rib 4; repeat from ★ ending last repeat, rib 4. [64 sts.]
Change to size "A" needles and with m. k. 1 row and p. 1 row. Now work from Chart A as follows:
1st to 10th rows: As given for sleeves of sweater.
11th row: With m. k.2, p.1, (k.3, p.1) twice, k.1, with b. k.1, with m. k.1, (p.1, k.3) 12 times, p.1, k.1.
12th row: With m. (k.3, p.1) 12 times, k.2, with b. p.1, k.1, p.1, with m. k.2, p.1, (p.3, k.1) twice.
The last 12 rows set the position of the pattern, given at the center of Chart A.
Continuing in pattern from chart, and working the extra sts. into the pattern as they occur, inc. 1 st. at each end of the next row and then every 3rd row 11 times. [88 sts.]
Now work the 8-row shell pattern, given for back of sweater.
With m. k. 1 row and p. 1 row.
Working the pattern from Chart A again, inc. 1 st. at each end of the next row and then every 3rd row 3 times. [96 sts.]
Work the 11th to 46th rows from Chart A, then work the first 8 rows again.
Bind off the remaining 96 sts.

Making Up

Do not press. Set in sleeves between the marking threads on back and front. Neatly sew one row end edge of each pocket back to each side of back, beginning just above the checked part of the pattern from Chart A. Join side seams, neatly catching pocket backs in place on wrong side of fronts. Join sleeve seams. Neatly sew button- and buttonhole bands in place. Sew on buttons.

a utumn
variations

Multicolor
Simple Sweater

ABOVE LEFT AND BELOW LEFT

One-color
Simple Sweater

RIGHT

Simple to knit, yet infinitely versatile, this sweater can
be made for all ages and all sizes, in one color or in a
variety of combinations.

PATTERN PAGE 30

a l p i n e

Subtle motifs of a tree, a house and a skier evoke memories of elegant alpine resorts and good times on the ski slopes.

A U T U M N

A l p i n e   S w e a t e r

PHOTOGRAPH THIS PAGE

Materials
12 50 gram balls of "Patricia Roberts Extra Thick Cotton." A pair each of size 3 and size 6 Aero knitting needles and a thick cable needle.

Color
Coral

Needle Sizes
Use size 6 needles for those referred to as size "A" and size 3 for those referred to as size "B".

W I N T E R

A l p i n e   S w e a t e r

PHOTOGRAPH PAGE 157

Materials
12 100 gram balls of "Patricia Roberts Extra Thick Wool." A pair each of size 5 and size 7 Aero knitting needles and a thick cable needle.

Color
Pink

Needle Sizes
Use size 7 needles for those referred to as size "A" and size 5 for those referred to as size "B".

Abbreviations
cable 12, thus, slip next 6 sts. onto a cable needle and leave at front of work, k.6, then k.6 from cable needle ■ **cr.2rt.**, cross 2 right thus, k. into back of 2nd st. on left-hand needle, then into front of first st. ■ **cr.2lt.**, cross 2 left thus, k. into front of 2nd st. on left-hand needle, then into back of first st. ■ **3 from 3**, thus, p.

AUTUMN

Alpine Sweater
RIGHT

WINTER

Alpine Sweater
PAGE 157

next 3 sts. tog. without dropping sts. from left-hand needle, y.r.n., then p. these 3 sts. tog. again ■ **m.b.**, make bobble thus, k.1, y.r.n., k.1 all into one st., turn, k.3, turn, p.3tog.

Tension

64 stitches, 1 repeat of the cable pattern, to 12 in (25 cm) in width and 24 rows to 3¼ in (8 cm) in depth, using size "A" needles.

Sweater Pattern

Measurements

Underarms: 54 in (135 cm). Side seam: 22 in (55 cm). Length: 32½ in (81 cm). Sleeve seam: 17 in (42.5 cm).

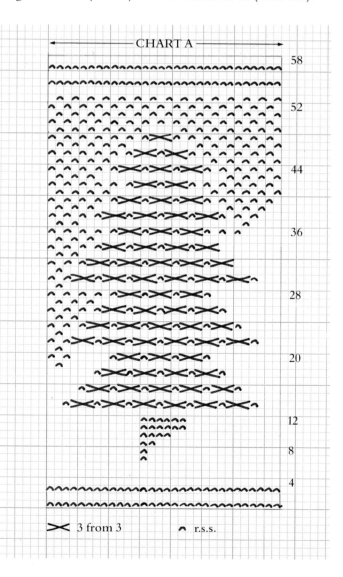

CHART A

58
52
44
36
28
20
12
8
4

✕ 3 from 3   ⌒ r.s.s.

Back

With size "B" needles cast on 144 sts. and work 24 rows in double rib.

Change to size "A" needles and work in cable pattern as follows:

1st row: P.2, ★ k.12, p.2 ★★, k.7, p.2, k.7, p.2; repeat from ★ ending last repeat at ★★.

2nd row: ★ P.16, k.1, p.14, k.1; repeat from ★ until 16 remain, p.16.

3rd row: ★ P.2, k.12, p.2 ★★, k.1, p.1, k.5, p.2, k.5, p.1, k.1; repeat from ★ ending last repeat at ★★.

4th row: ★ P.16, k.1, p.1, k.1, p.10, k.1, p.1, k.1; repeat from ★ until 16 remain, p.16.

5th row: ★ P.2, k.12, p.2 ★★, k.1, p.1, k.1, p.1, k.3, p.2, k.3, p.1, k.1, p.1, k.1; repeat from ★ ending last repeat at ★★.

6th row: ★ p.16, k.1, (p.1, k.1) twice, p.6, (k.1, p.1) twice, k.1; repeat from ★ until 16 remain, p.16.

7th row: ★ P.2, cable 12, p.2 ★★, k.1, (p.1, k.1) 3 times, p.2, k.1, (p.1, k.1) 3 times; repeat from ★ ending last repeat at ★★.

8th row: As 6th row.

9th to 12th rows: Work the 5th row back to the 2nd row.

13th to 24th rows: As 1st to 12th rows.

25th to 30th rows: As 1st to 6th rows.

31st row: ★ P.2, k.12, p.2 ★★, k.1, (p.1, k.1) 3 times, p.2, k.1, (p.1, k.1) 3 times, p.2, cable 12, p.2, k.1, (p.1, k.1) 3 times, p.2, k.1, (p.1, k.1) 3 times, ★; repeat from ★ to ★ once, then from ★ to ★★.

32nd to 36th rows: As 8th to 12th rows.

The last 36 rows form the cable pattern. Work the first 2 rows again.

Now continuing in cable pattern as set, inset the patterns from the charts as follows:

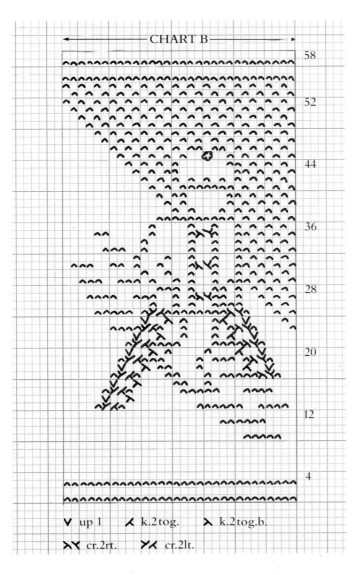

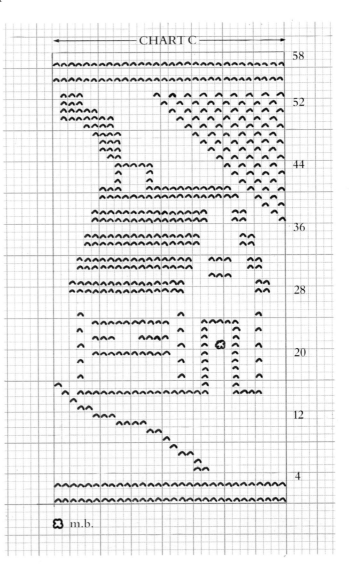

** *Next row*: Work in cable pattern as set across 25 sts., then work as given for first row of Chart A across the next 30 sts. Work 34 sts. in cable pattern as set, then work as given for first row of Chart B over the next 30 sts.; work to end in cable pattern.

Next row: Work 25 sts. in cable pattern, then 30 sts. from 2nd row of Chart B, cable pattern 34, then pattern 30 sts. as given for 2nd row of Chart A, cable pattern 25 sts. **

The last 2 rows set the position of the patterns given in the charts. Now work the 3rd to 58th rows as set. Work 38 rows in cable pattern.

Reading Chart B for Chart A and Chart C for Chart B, work from ** to **. Continuing in cable pattern with the patterns from Charts B and C as set, work 2 rows.

To shape the armholes: Continuing in cable pattern, with patterns from the charts as set, bind off 10 sts. at the beginning of the next 2 rows, then dec. 1 st. at each end of the next row and the 12 following alternate rows. ★★★

On 98 sts. pattern 27 rows to complete the patterns from the charts. Work 24 rows in cable pattern.

To slope the shoulders: Bind off 28 sts. at the beginning of the next 2 rows.

Bind off the remaining 42 sts.

Front

Work as given for back until ★★★ is reached.

Pattern 26 rows as set.

Now divide the sts. for the neck:

Next row: Pattern 40 and leave these sts. on a spare needle until required for right front shoulder, bind off 18 sts. for the neck, pattern to end and continue on these sts. for the left front shoulder.

Left front shoulder: To shape the neck: Dec. 1 st. at the neck edge on the next 12 rows.

On 28 sts. pattern 12 rows.

To slope the shoulder: Bind off.

Right front shoulder: With right side of work facing rejoin yarn to inner edge of sts. left on spare needle and work to end of row, then work as given for left front shoulder to end.

Collar

With size "B" needles cast on 108 sts. and work 46 rows in double rib, then bind off very loosely, using a size larger needle.

Sleeves

Both alike: With size "B" needles cast on 48 sts. and work 20 rows in double rib.

Change to size "A" needles and work the first 12 cable pattern rows as given for back. These 12 rows form the repeat pattern for the sleeves.

Maintaining the continuity of the pattern and working the extra sts. into the pattern as they occur, inc. 1 st. at each end of the next row and then every 4th row 24 times. On 98 sts. pattern 7 rows.

To shape the sleeve top: Bind off 10 sts. at the beginning of the next 2 rows, then dec. 1 st. at each end of the next row and the 8 following alternate rows, then at each end of the next 5 rows. Bind off 5 sts. at the beginning of the next 8 rows. Bind off the remaining 10 sts.

Making Up

Do not press. Join shoulder seams. Set in sleeves. Join sleeve and side seams. Join row ends of collar for 1 in (2.5 cm) on Autumn Sweater or completely on Winter Sweater. Neatly sew *bound off* edge in place all round neck edge with seam to center front on Autumn Sweater or to left front shoulder on Winter Sweater.

autumn variations

Abstract Cardigan

LEFT
Dynamic abstract shapes crisscross this chunky wool cardigan with its deeply cut neck.
PATTERN PAGE 20

Short Twist Sweater

ABOVE RIGHT
Blue and white stripes give a nautical feel to this cropped cotton version of the Twist design.
PATTERN PAGE 132

Angel Fish Sweater

BELOW RIGHT
Autumnal blues and greens make this wool version of the Angel Fish design strikingly different from its summer alternatives.
PATTERN PAGE 74

_w_ inter

In this festive season there is no need to sacrifice excitement and style for warmth and practicality. The winter designs combine these elements perfectly, with stunning colors, truly original motifs and patterning and more than a hint of luxury in materials which include angora and lambswool. Black, red and pink, dominant in Patchwork Roses, Raj and Tea Rose, will cheer up the darkest winter's day. Bright blue lambswool in Twist and subtle sand or gray in Spaghetti show up the dramatic cable patterning to full effect and although they look complex, these designs are in fact based on a simple cable stitch.

FROM LEFT TO RIGHT:
PATCHWORK ROSES JACKET, TWIST SWEATER, SPAGHETTI
SWEATER, RAJ CARDIGAN AND TEA ROSE T-SHIRT

patchwork roses

Full-blown roses climbing a trellis were the inspiration for this versatile jacket and vest scattered with bold floral motifs.

WINTER

Patchwork Roses Jacket

PHOTOGRAPH THIS PAGE

Materials
20 25 gram balls of "Patricia Roberts Angora" in main color and, in the same yarn, 3 balls in each of the contrasts b. and g., 2 balls in contrast c. and 1 ball in each of the contrasts e. and f.; plus 4 50 gram balls of "Patricia Roberts Pure Wool No.2" in contrast a. and 2 25 gram balls of "Patricia Roberts Pure Wool No.1" in contrast d. A pair each of size 2 and size 3 Aero knitting needles and 7 buttons.

Colors
m. = black angora, a. = black wool, b. = red,
c. = green, d. = khaki, e. = yellow, f. = orange,
g. = geranium.

Needle Sizes
Use size 3 needles for those referred to as size "A" and size 2 needles for those referred to as size "B" in the pattern.

WINTER

Patchwork Roses Vest

PHOTOGRAPH THIS PAGE

Materials
13 25 gram balls of "Patricia Roberts Angora" in main color and, in the same yarn, 2 balls in each of the contrasts b., c. and g. and 1 ball in each of the contrasts e. and f.; plus 4 50 gram balls of "Patricia Roberts Pure

WINTER

Patchwork Roses Jacket
ABOVE RIGHT AND OPPOSITE

Patchwork Roses Vest
BELOW RIGHT

SPRING

Patchwork Roses Jacket
PAGE 29

SUMMER

Patchwork Roses Vest
PAGE 83

Wool No.2" in contrast a. and 1 25 gram ball of "Patricia Roberts Pure Wool No.1" in contrast d. A pair each of size 2 and size 3 Aero knitting needles and 7 buttons.

Colors
m. = red angora, a. = red wool, b. = shocking pink, c. = green, d. = olive wool, e. = orange, f. = yellow, g. = cherry.

Needle Sizes
Use size 3 needles for those referred to as size "A" and size 2 for those referred to as size "B" in the pattern.

SPRING

Patchwork Roses Jacket

PHOTOGRAPH PAGE 29

Materials
26 25 gram balls of "Patricia Roberts Fine Cotton" in main color and 3 balls of the same yarn in contrast g.; plus 3 50 gram balls of "Patricia Roberts Cotton No.2" in contrast b. and 1 ball in each of the contrasts c., d., e. and f. A pair each of size 2 and size 3 Aero knitting needles and 7 buttons.

Colors
m. = pink, b. = shocking pink, c. = khaki, d. = mauve, e. = coral, f. = yellow, g. = red.

Needle Sizes
Use size 3 needles for those referred to as size "A" and size 2 for those referred to as size "B" in the pattern.

SUMMER

Patchwork Roses Vest

PHOTOGRAPH PAGE 83

Materials
20 25 gram balls of "Patricia Roberts Fine Cotton" in main color and 2 balls of the same yarn in contrast g.; plus 2 50 gram balls of "Patricia Roberts Cotton No.2"

in contrast b. and 1 ball in each of the contrasts c., d., e. and f. A pair each of size 2 and size 3 Aero knitting needles and 8 buttons.

Colors
m. = white, b. = mauve, c. = khaki, d. and e. = sand, f. = yellow, g. = pink.

Needle Sizes
Use size 3 needles for those referred to as size "A" and size 2 for those referred to as size "B" in the pattern.

Abbreviations
36 from 24, (k.1, inc. in next st.) 12 times ■ **m.k.,** make knot thus on wrong side rows, with d., p.1, slip the st. just made back to left-hand needle and k. this st.

Winter Jacket & Vest Pattern

Tension
Based on a stockinette stitch tension of 14 stitches and 18 rows to 2 in (5 cm) using size "A" needles, one rectangular patch of the pattern will measure 4½ in (11 cm) in width and 4¼ in (10.5 cm) in depth.

Measurements
Jacket
Underarms: 46½ in (116 cm). Side seam: 22¼ in (55.5 cm).
Length: 31 in (77.5 cm). Sleeve seam: 17 in (42.5 cm).
Vest
Underarms: 46½ in (116 cm). Side seam: 18 in (45 cm).
Length: 26¾ in (67 cm).

Back
Center back panel: With size "B" needles and a. cast on 55 sts. and work 10 rows in single rib. Break off a., join in m.
Change to size "A" needles and work in pattern as follows. Use separate small balls of color for each section of the pattern, so that colors not in use are not taken across the back of the work.
1st row: With m. all k.
2nd row: With m. all p.
3rd and 4th rows: As 1st and 2nd rows.
5th row: With m. k.2, 36 from 24, k.3, 36 from 24, k.2.
6th row: With m. p.17, with c. p.2, with m. p. to end.
7th row: With m, k.2, then k.36, turn, p.36, turn, k.36, then k.3, now working from chart A with m. k.18,

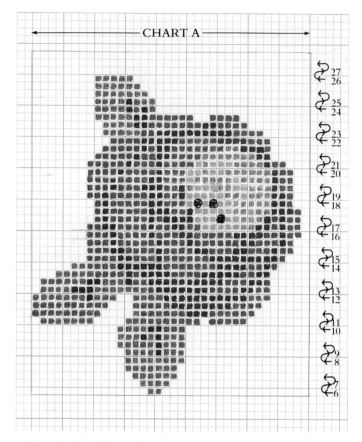

CHART A

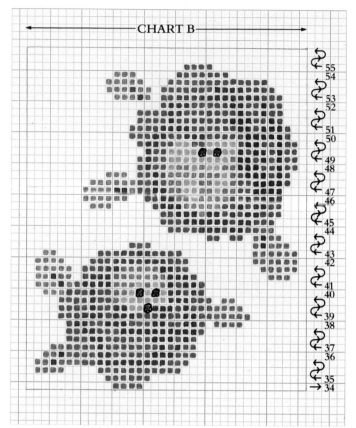

CHART B

with c. k.4, with m. k.14, turn, with m. p.13, with c. p.6, with m. p.17, turn, with m. k.17, with c. k.7, with m. k.12, then k.2.

8th row: With m. p.2, working from Chart A with m. p.12, with c. p.8, with m. p. to end.

9th to 27th rows: Continuing to work in turning rows on every right side row as given for the 7th row, continue in pattern from Chart A as set.

28th row: With m. p.2, ★ (p.2tog., p.1) 12 times, p.3; repeat from ★ ending p.2.

29th to 33rd rows: As 1st to 5th rows.

34th row: With m. p.2, then p.36, then p.3, then p.11, with b. p.4, with m. p.21, then p.2.

35th row: With m. k.2, working from Chart B with m. k.20, with b. k.6, with m. k.10, turn, with m. p.1, with c. p.4, with m. p.4, with b. p.11, with m. p.16, turn, with m. k.15, with b. k.3, with g. k.9, with m. k.2, with c. k.3, with d. k.1, with c. k.2, with m. k.1, then k.3, then k.36, turn, p.36, turn, k.36, then k.2.

36th row: With m. p.2, then p.36, then p.3, work as given for 36th row of Chart B across next 36 sts., with m. p.2.

37th to 55th rows: Continuing to work in turning rows on every right side row, work in pattern from Chart B as set.

56th row: As 28th row.

57th to 61st rows: As 1st to 5th rows.

62nd row: With m. p.2, then p.8, with c. p.1, with m. p.18, with c. p.1, with m. p.8, then p.3, then p.36, then p.2.

63rd row: With m. k.2, then k.36, turn, p.36, turn, k.36, then k.3, now working from Chart C with m. k.7, with c. k.3, with m. k.16, with c. k.3, with m. k.7, turn, p.7, with c. p.3, with m. p.16, with c. p.3, with m. p.3, with c. p.2, with m. p.2, turn, k.2, with c. k.3, with m. k.2, with c. k.3, with m. k.11, with c. k.3, with m. k.3, with d. k.1, with m. k.8, then k.2.

64th row: With m. p.2, work from Chart C across next 36 sts., with m. p. to end.

65th to 83rd rows: Continuing to work in turning rows on every right side row, work in pattern from Chart C as set.

84th row: As 28th row.

85th to 89th rows: As 1st to 5th rows.

90th row: With m. p.2, then p.36, then p.3, working from chart A with m. p.15, with c. p.2, with m. p.19, then p.2.

91st to 168th rows: As 7th to 84th rows, but exchanging the position of the plain squares with the patterned squares.

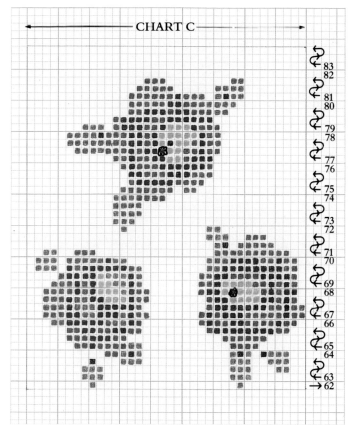

CHART C

83 82 81 80 79 78 77 76 75 74 73 72 71 70 69 68 67 66 65 64 63 62

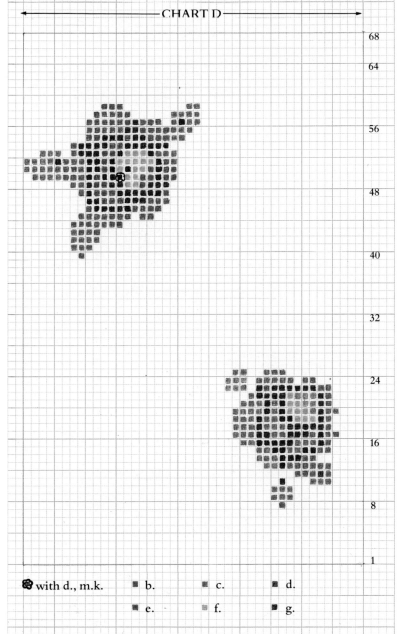

CHART D

68 64 56 48 40 32 24 16 8 1

The last 168 rows form the pattern.
For the Winter Jacket:
Work the first 30 rows again.
For the Winter Vest:
Work the first 2 rows again.
For both versions:
Bind off loosely the 55 sts.
Right half back: Work as given for center back panel, until 140 rows have been worked in pattern for the Winter Jacket or 112 rows have been worked for the Winter Vest. Work 1 extra row here, when working left half back.
★★To shape the armhole: Continue in pattern as follows. Marking the 14th st. with a colored thread, bind off 27 sts. at the beginning of the next row. Pattern 57 rows. Work 1 row less here on left half back. Bind off the remaining 28 sts.
Left half back: Work as given for right half back, noting the variations in the number of rows.

L e f t   F r o n t
For the Winter Jacket: Work as given for center back panel until 169 pattern rows have been worked, marking the beginning of the 141st row with a colored thread to denote armhole.

★ with d., m.k.　■ b.　■ c.　■ d.
■ e.　□ f.　■ g.

For the Winter Vest:
Work as given for center back panel, until 141 rows have been worked in pattern, marking the beginning of the 113th row with a colored thread to denote armhole.
★★★For both versions:
To shape the neck: Bind off 16 sts. at the beginning of the next row, then dec. 1 st. at the neck edge on the next 2 rows.
Next row: With m. k.2, then 36 from 24, then k.9, k.2tog.

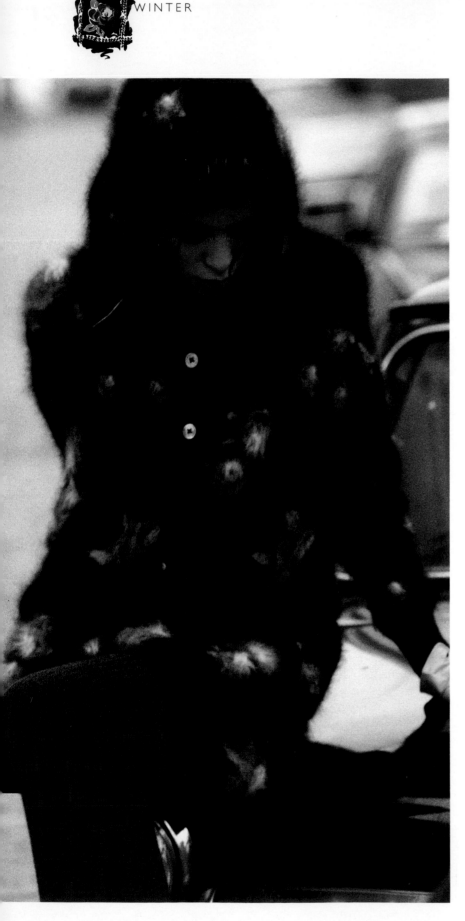

Next row: With m. p.2tog., p. to end.
Continuing in turning row pattern, dec. 1 st. at the neck edge on each of the next 7 rows.
Pattern 17 rows.
To slope the shoulder: Bind off the 28 remaining sts.

Right Front

For the Winter Jacket:
Work as given for center back panel until the 168 pattern rows have been worked, marking the beginning of the 140th row with a colored thread to denote armhole.

For the Winter Vest:
Work as given for center back panel, until 140 rows have been worked in pattern, marking the beginning of the 112th row with a colored thread to denote armhole.

***For both versions:
To shape the neck: Bind off 16 sts. at the beginning of the next row, work 1 row back to neck edge, then dec. 1 st. at the neck edge on each of the next 2 rows.
Next row: With m. k.2tog., k.9, 36 from 24, k.2.
Next row: Pattern as set until 2 remain, p.2tog.
Continuing in this way in pattern from appropriate chart, dec. 1 st. at the neck edge on each of the next 7 rows.
Pattern 17 rows as set.
To slope the shoulder: Bind off the 28 remaining sts.

Frontbands

Buttonband: With size "B" needles and a. cast on 10 sts. and work 180 rows in single rib for the Winter Jacket or 156 rows for the Winter Vest, then bind off.

Buttonhole band: With size "B" needles and a. cast on 10 sts. and work 6 rows in single rib.
**1st Buttonhole row: Rib 3, bind off 4, rib to end.
2nd Buttonhole row: Rib 3, turn, cast on 4, turn, rib to end.
Rib 26 rows for the Winter Jacket or 22 rows for the Winter Vest.**
Repeat from ** to ** 5 times more, then work the 2 buttonhole rows again.
Rib 4 rows, then bind off in rib.

Hood

First half: With size "B" needles and a. cast on 132 stitches and work 10 rows in single rib. Break off a., join in m.
Change to size "A" needles and work in pattern from Chart D as follows, noting information given for color work at beginning of pattern.

1st to 7th rows: With m. in s.s.

8th row: With the wrong side of work facing and m. p.33, ★ with c. p.1, with m. p.43; repeat from ★ ending last repeat with m. p.10.

9th row: With m. k.9, ★ with c. k.3, with m. k.41; repeat from ★ ending last repeat k.32.

10th row: With m. p.32, ★ with c. p.3, with m. p.41; repeat from ★, ending last repeat with m. p.9.

The last 10 rows set the position of the pattern, given in Chart D. Work the 11th to 68th rows as set. Work 1 extra row here when working second half.

To shape the hood: Maintaining the continuity of the pattern bind off 2 sts. at the beginning of the next row and the 13 following alternate rows, then bind off 8 sts. on the 4 following alternate rows.

On 72 sts. work 1 row, then bind off.

Second half: Work as given for first half, noting the variation in the rows.

Sleeves

For the Winter Jacket:

Both alike: With size "B" needles and a. cast on 56 sts. and work 23 rows in single rib.

Increase row: Rib 3, ★ up 1, rib 7; repeat from ★ ending last repeat rib 4 [64 sts.]. Break off m., join in a. Change to size "A" needles and work in pattern from Chart D, noting information given for color work at beginning of pattern.

1st to 7th rows: With m. beginning with a k. row s.s. 7 rows.

8th row: With m. p.9, with c. p.1, with m. p.43, with c. p.1, with m. p.10.

9th row: With m. k.9, with c. k.3, with m. k.41, with c. k.3, with m. k.8.

10th row: With m. p.8, with c. p.3, with m. p.41, with c. p.3, with m. p.9.

The last 10 rows set the position of the 44-st. repeat pattern given in Chart D. Now work the 11th to 16th rows from the chart as set.

Continuing in the 68-row repeat pattern as set and working the extra sts. into the pattern as they occur, inc. 1 st. at each end of the next row and then every 4th row 23 times.

On 112 sts. pattern 19 rows.

Mark each end of the last row with colored threads. Pattern 18 rows more.

To shape the sleeve top: Dec. 1 st. at each end of the next 8 rows. Then bind off 6 sts. at the beginning of the next 8 rows.

Bind off loosely the remaining 48 sts.

Armbands

For the Winter Vest:

Both alike: First join shoulder seams. With right side of work facing, rejoin a. and using size "B" needles, pick up and k. 154 sts. from all round armhole edge. Work 7 rows in single rib, then bind off in rib.

Pocket backs

Both alike: With size "A" needles and m. cast on 36 sts. and work 46 rows in s.s., then bind off.

Making Up

Do not press. Join left and right half backs to center back panel. Join side seams, inserting pocket backs above the first patchwork squares, neatly sewing them in place behind fronts.

For the Winter Jacket:

Join shoulder seams. Join sleeve seams up to marking threads. Then matching marking threads on sleeves to those on left and right half back panels, set in sleeves, so that the row ends above the marking threads on the sleeves are sewn to the bound-off sts. at each side of the marking threads.

For both versions:

Join shaped row ends and bound off edges of half hood pieces. Sew button- and buttonhole bands in place. Sew straight row end edges of hood in place all around neck edge, including frontbands. Sew on buttons.

Spring Jacket Pattern

Tension
Based on a stockinette stitch tension of 13 stitches and 17 rows to 2 in (5 cm), and using size "A" needles, one rectangular patch of the pattern will measure 4⅞ in (12 cm) in width and 4½ in (11 cm) in depth.

Measurements
Underarms; 48½ in (121 cm). Side seam: 19 in (47.5 cm). Length: 28½ in (71 cm). Sleeve seam: 17 in (42.5 cm).

Back, Left and Right Fronts, Pocket Backs and Hood
Using m. instead of a., work as given for Winter Vest.

Frontbands
Buttonband: With size "B" needles and m. cast on 10 sts. and work 230 rows in single rib, then bind off.
Buttonhole band: With size "B" needles and m. cast on 10 sts. and work 8 rows in single rib.
★★1st Buttonhole row: Rib 3, bind off 4, rib to end.
2nd Buttonhole row: Rib 3, turn, cast on 4, turn, rib to end.
Rib 34 rows.★★
Repeat from ★★ to ★★ 5 times more, then work the 2 buttonhole rows again.
Rib 4 rows, then bind off in rib.

Sleeves
Both alike: Using m. instead of a. and working 9 rows instead of 19 before placing the marking threads, work as given for sleeves of Winter Jacket.

Making Up
As given for Winter Jacket.

Summer Vest Pattern

Tension
Based on a stockinette stitch tension of 13 stitches and 17 rows to 2 in (5 cm), and using size "A" needles, one rectangular patch of the pattern will measure 4⅞ in (12 cm) in width and 4½ in (11 cm) in depth.

Measurements
Underarms: 48½ in (121 cm). Side seam: 16¼ (41 cm). Length: 25 in (62.5 cm).

Back
Center back panel: With size "B" needles and m. cast on 55 sts. and work 26 rows in single rib.
Change to size "A" needles and work the first 144 pattern rows given for back of Winter Jacket, then bind off.
Right half back: Work as given for center panel, until 84 rows have been worked in pattern. Work 1 extra row here on left half back.
Work as given for right half back of Winter Jacket from ★★ to end.

Left Front
Work as given for center back panel until 113 pattern rows have been worked, marking the beginning of the

85th row with a colored thread to denote the armhole.
Now work as given for left front of Winter Jacket from ★★★ to end.

Right Front

Work as given for center back panel until 112 pattern rows have been worked, marking the beginning of the 84th row with a colored thread to denote armhole.
Now work as given for right front of Winter Jacket from ★★★ to end.

Pocket Backs, Hood and Armbands

Using m. instead of a., work as given for Winter Vest.

Frontbands

Buttonband: With size "B" needles and m. cast on 10 sts. and work 206 rows in single rib, then bind off.
Buttonhole band: With size "B" needles and m. cast on 10 sts. and work 6 rows in single rib.
** *1st Buttonhole row*: Rib 4, bind off 2, rib to end.
2nd Buttonhole row: Rib 4, turn, cast on 2, turn, rib to end.
Rib 26 rows.**
Repeat from ** to ** 6 times more, then work the 2 buttonhole rows again.
Rib 2 rows, then bind off in rib.

Making Up

As given for Winter Vest.

t w i s t

Two styles of cabling distinguish this long sweater and its cropped autumn version.

W I N T E R

Long Twist Sweater

PHOTOGRAPH THIS PAGE

Materials
Either 17 50 gram balls of "Patricia Roberts Geelong Lambswool No.2" or 23 50 gram balls of "Patricia Roberts Pure Wool No.2." A pair each of size 5 and size 6 Aero knitting needles and a medium-size cable needle.

Colors
Lambswool: blue; Pure Wool: cream.

Needle Sizes
Use size 6 needles for those referred to as size "A" and size 5 for those referred to as size "B" in the pattern.

A U T U M N

Short Twist Sweater

PHOTOGRAPH PAGE 119

Materials
10 50 gram balls of "Patricia Roberts Cotton No.2" in main color and 8 balls of the same yarn, in a contrasting color. A pair each of size 5 and size 3 Aero knitting needles and a medium-size cable needle.

Colors
m. = navy, a. = white.

Needle Sizes
Use size 5 needles for those referred to as size "A" and size 3 needles for those referred to as size "B" in the pattern.

Abbreviations
c.12f., cable 12 front thus, slip next 6 sts. onto a cable needle and leave at front of work, k.6, then k.6 from

WINTER

Long Twist Sweater
RIGHT AND
PAGE 141

AUTUMN

Short Twist Sweater
PAGE 119

cable needle ■ **c.12b.**, cable 12 back thus, slip next 6 sts. onto cable needle at back of work, k.6, then k.6 from cable needle ■ **c.6f.**, cable 6 front thus, slip next 3 sts. onto cable needle at front of work, k.3, then k.3 from cable needle ■ **c.6b.**, cable 6 back thus, slip next 3 sts. onto cable needle at back of work, k.3, then k.3 from cable needle.

Tension

24 stitches, 1 repeat of the pattern, to 2¾ in (7 cm) and 40 rows, 2 repeats of the pattern, to 5 in (12.5 cm) over the main pattern using size "A" needles.

Long Sweater Pattern

Measurements

Underarms: 47 in (118 cm). Side seam: 19¼ in (48 cm). Length: 30¼ in (75.5 cm). Sleeve seam: 17 in (42.5 cm).

Back

With size "B" needles cast on 206 sts. and work 14 rows in double rib. Change to size "A" needles and work in pattern as follows:

1st row: All k.
2nd row: K.1, p. until 1 remains, k.1.
3rd to 8th rows: Repeat 1st and 2nd rows 4 times.
9th row: K.1, k.12, ★ c.12f., k.12; repeat from ★ ending last repeat k.1 more.
10th row: As 2nd row.
11th to 18th rows: Repeat 1st and 2nd rows 4 times.
19th row: K.1, c.12b., ★ k.12, c.12b.; repeat from ★ ending last repeat k.1 more.
20th row: As 2nd row.
The last 20 rows form the pattern. Repeat them 6 times more.
To shape the armholes: Maintaining the continuity of the pattern as set, bind off 6 sts. at the beginning of the next 2 rows, then dec. 1 st. at each end of the next row and the 5 following alternate rows. [182 sts.]
Work 20 rows in pattern as set.
***Increase row*: K.1, p.10, ★ up 1, p.8; repeat from ★ ending last repeat p.10, k.1. [203 sts.]
Now work in cable rib pattern as follows:
1st row: K.2, p.2, k.6, p.2, k.2, ★ p.2, k.9, p.2, k.2, p.2, k.6, p.2, k.2; repeat from ★ to end.
2nd row: K.1, p.1, ★ k.2, p.6, k.2, p.2, k.2, p.9, k.2, p.2; repeat from ★ until 12 sts. remain, k.2, p.6, k.2, p.1, k.1.
3rd row: K.2, p.2, k.6, p.2, k.2, ★ p.2, c.6f., k.3, p.2,

k.2, p.2, k.6, p.2, k.2; repeat from ★ to end.
4th row: As 2nd row.
5th row: K.2, p.2, c.6f., p.2, k.2, ★ p.2, k.9, p.2, k.2, p.2, c.6f., p.2, k.2; repeat from ★ to end.
6th row: As 2nd row.
7th row: K.2, p.2, k.6, p.2, k.2, ★ p.2, k.3, c.6b., p.2, k.2, p.2, k.6, p.2, k.2; repeat from ★ to end.
8th row: As 2nd row.
The last 8 rows form the cable rib pattern. ★★
Repeat these 8 rows 5 times more.
To slope the shoulders: Continuing in pattern, bind off 21 sts. at the beginning of the next 6 rows.
Bind off the remaining 77 sts. loosely.

Front

Work as given for back until ★★ is reached. Work 11 rows more in cable rib.
Now divide the sts. for the neck:
Next row: Continuing in cable rib, pattern 88 sts. and leave these sts. on a spare needle until required for right front shoulder, bind off 27 sts. for the neck, pattern to end and continue on these 88 sts. for the left front shoulder.
Left front shoulder: To shape the neck: Dec. 1 st. at the neck edge on each of the next 25 rows.
On 63 sts. pattern 3 rows.
To slope the shoulder: Bind off 21 sts. at the beginning of the next row and the following alternate row. On 21 sts. work 1 row, then bind off.
Right front shoulder: With right side of work facing rejoin yarn to inner edge of the 88 sts. left on spare needle and work to end of row, then work as given for left front shoulder to end.
Collar: First join right shoulder seam. With right side of work facing rejoin yarn to left front shoulder and using size "B" needles, pick up and k. 34 sts. from left front neck edge, 26 sts. from center front neck, 34 sts. from right front neck edge and 76 sts. from back neck edge. On 170 sts. work 60 rows in double rib.
Bind off loosely using a size larger needle.

Sleeves

Both alike: With size "B" needles cast on 68 sts. and work the 8-row cable rib pattern given for back 4 times, then work the 1st row again.
Increase row: K.1, p.1, ★ up 1, p.2, up 1, p.1; repeat from ★ until 3 remain, p.2, k.1. [110 sts.]
★★ Change to size "A" needles and work the 20-row main pattern given for back.
Maintaining the continuity of the pattern and working the extra sts. in as they occur, inc. 1 st. at each end of the next row and then every 4th row 20 times.

On 152 sts. pattern 3 rows.
To shape the sleeve top: Bind off 6 sts. at the beginning of the next 2 rows, then dec. 1 st. at each end of the next row and the 5 following alternate rows. On 128 sts. work 1 row. Bind off loosely.

Making Up

Do not press. Join left shoulder seam, continuing seam across collar. Set in sleeves. Join sleeve and side seams.

Short Sweater Pattern

Measurements

Underarms: 47 in (118 cm). Side seam: 9¼ in (23 cm). Length: 20 in (50 cm). Sleeve seam: 17 in (42.5 cm).

Back

With size "B" needles and a. cast on 206 sts. and work 14 rows in double rib.
Change to size "A" needles and work in main pattern as given for back of Long Sweater Pattern, but in stripes as follows:
1st to 4th rows: In a.
5th to 14th rows: In m.
15th to 20th rows: In a.
Repeat the 20-row striped cable pattern twice more.
To shape the armholes: Continuing in pattern, bind off 6 sts. at the beginning of the next 2 rows; then dec. 1 st. at each end of the next row and the 5 following alternate rows.
Work 19 rows in stripe pattern as before.
Continuing with m. only, k. 1 row then work as given for Long Sweater Pattern from ★★★ to end.

Front

Work as given for back until ★★ is reached, then work as given for front of Long Sweater Pattern to end.
Neckband: With m. work as given for collar of Long Sweater Pattern, but working 9 rows in double rib instead of 60.
Bind off loosely in rib.

Sleeves

Both alike: With a., work as given for sleeves of Long Sweater Pattern until the increase row has been worked. Now working in striped cable pattern as for back, work as given for sleeves of Long Sweater Pattern from ★★ to end.

Making Up

As for Long Sweater Pattern.

winter variations

Bobbles Jacket

BELOW
Cream wool gives a luxurious feel to this version of the hooded Bobbles design.
PATTERN PAGE 70

Thin Bears Sweater

RIGHT
Polar bear motifs, knitted in angora, are interspersed between the cables on this roll-neck sweater with a strong seasonal note.
PATTERN PAGE 92

s p a g h e t t i

The effect of this design is quite dramatic, but in fact the simple cable stitch used throughout makes it straightforward to knit. It is chunky and comfortable enough to be worn by a man or a woman.

W I N T E R

S p a g h e t t i   S w e a t e r
PHOTOGRAPH THIS PAGE

Materials
12 100 gram balls of "Patricia Roberts Extra Thick Wool." A pair each of size 6 and size 8 Aero knitting needles and a large cable needle.

Colors
Sand or gray.

Needle Sizes
Use size 8 needles for those referred to as size "A" and size 6 needles for those referred to as size "B" in the pattern.

Abbreviations
c.12f., cable 12 front thus, slip next 6 sts. onto a cable needle and leave at front of work, k.6, then k.6 from cable needle ■ c.12b., cable 12 back thus, slip next 6 sts. onto cable needle at back of work, k.6, then k.6 from cable needle.

Tension
24 stitches, 1 repeat of the pattern, to 3¼ in (9 cm) and 20 rows, 1 repeat of the pattern, to 3 in (7.5 cm) over the pattern using size "A" needles.

S w e a t e r   P a t t e r n

Measurements
Underarms: 46 in (115 cm). Side seam: 15 in (37.5 cm). Length: 26 in (65 cm). Sleeve seam: 19 in (47.5 cm).

Back
With size "B" needles cast on 170 sts. and work 20 rows in double rib.

WINTER

Spaghetti Sweater
RIGHT

Change to size "A" needles and work in pattern as follows:

1st row: All k.

2nd row: K.1, p. until 1 remains, k.1.

3rd to 8th rows: Repeat 1st and 2nd rows 4 times.

9th row: K.1, ★ c.12f., k.12; repeat from ★ ending last repeat k.1 more.

10th row: As 2nd row.

11th to 18th rows: Repeat 1st and 2nd rows 4 times.

19th row: K.1, ★ k.12, c.12b.; repeat from ★ ending last repeat k.1 more.

20th row: As 2nd row.

The last 20 rows form the pattern, repeat them 3 times more. Mark each end of the last row with colored threads to denote armholes. ★★

Work 70 rows more in pattern as set.

To slope the shoulders: Continuing in pattern, bind off 29 sts. at the beginning of the next 4 rows.

Bind off the remaining 54 sts. loosely.

Front

Work as given for back until ★★ is reached.

Work 47 rows more in cable rib.

Now divide the sts. for the neck:

Next row: With wrong side of work facing k.1, p.71, and leave these 72 sts. on a spare needle until required for right front shoulder, bind off 26 sts. for the neck, work to end and continue on these 72 sts. for the left front shoulder.

Left front shoulder: To shape the neck: Continuing in pattern dec. 1 st. at the neck edge on each of the next 14 rows. On 58 sts. pattern 8 rows.

To slope the shoulder: Bind off 29 sts. at the beginning of the next row. On 29 sts. work 1 row, then bind off.

Right front shoulder: With right side of work facing rejoin yarn to inner edge of the 72 sts. left on spare needle and work to end of row, then work as given for left front shoulder to end.

Collar: First join right shoulder seam. With right side of work facing rejoin yarn to left front shoulder and using size "B" needles, pick up and k. 26 sts. from left front neck edge, 26 sts. from center front neck, 26 sts. from right front neck edge and 54 sts. from back neck edge. On 132 sts. work 48 rows in double rib. Bind off loosely in rib using a size larger needle.

Sleeves

Both alike: With size "B" needles cast on 50 sts. and work 23 rows in double rib.

Increase row: P.2, ★ up 1, p.1; repeat from ★ to end. [98 sts.]

Change to size "A" needles and work the 20-row main pattern given for back.

Maintaining the continuity of the pattern and working the extra sts. into the pattern as they occur, inc. 1 st. at each end of the next row and then every 4th row 20 times. On 140 sts. pattern 5 rows, then bind off loosely.

Making Up

Do not press. Join left shoulder seam, continuing seam across collar. Set in sleeves. Join sleeve and side seams.

Below THE WOMAN IS WEARING THE TWIST SWEATER (PAGE 132).

r a j

This Indian-inspired design has long and short versions of both the cardigan and sweater and can be knitted in warm wool for winter or fine cotton for summer.

WINTER

Short Raj Sweater

PHOTOGRAPH THIS PAGE

Materials
24 25 gram balls of "Patricia Roberts Pure Wool No.1" in main color, and 1 25 gram ball of "Patricia Roberts Angora" in each of the contrasts a., b., c., d., e., f., g. and j.; plus small amounts of "Patricia Roberts Angora" in each of the contrasts i., l. and n. and 1 25 gram ball of "Patricia Roberts Pure Wool No.1" in h. A pair each of size 2 and size 3 Aero knitting needles and a fine cable needle.

Colors
m. = airforce blue, a. = shocking pink, b. = yellow, c. = rust, d. = mauve, e. = orient blue, f. = peacock blue, g. = pink, h. = green, i. = dark gray, j. = mid gray, l. = white, n. = black.

Needle Sizes
Use size 3 needles for those referred to as size "A" and size 2 needles for those referred to as size "B" in the pattern.

WINTER

Short Raj Cardigan

PHOTOGRAPH THIS PAGE

Materials
24 25 gram balls of "Patricia Roberts Pure Wool No.1" in main color, 1 50 gram ball of "Patricia Roberts Chenille" in each of the contrasts a., b., c., d., e., f. and g. and 1 50 gram ball of "Patricia Roberts Pure Wool No.2" in contrast h.; plus small amounts of "Patricia Roberts Pure Wool No.2" in contrasts l. and n., 1 25 gram ball of "Patricia Roberts Angora" in contrast j. and a small amount in contrast i. A pair each of size 3 and size 5 Aero knitting needles, a fine cable needle and 7 buttons.

WINTER

Short Raj Cardigan
ABOVE RIGHT, BELOW RIGHT AND OPPOSITE

Short Raj Sweater
CENTER RIGHT

SUMMER

Long Raj Cardigan
PAGE 63

Long Raj Sweater
PAGE 82

Colors

m. = black, a. = shocking pink, b. = yellow, c. = rust, d. = violet, e. = blue, f. = peacock blue, g. = red, h. = green, i. = dark gray, j. = mid gray, l. = white, n. = black.

Needle Sizes

Use size 5 needles for those referred to as size "A" and size 3 needles for those referred to as size "B" in the pattern.

SUMMER

Long Raj Sweater

PHOTOGRAPH PAGE 82

Materials

24 25 gram balls of "Patricia Roberts Fine Cotton" in main color, and 1 50 gram ball of "Patricia Roberts Cotton No.2" in each of the contrasts a., b., c., d., e., f., g. and h.; plus small amounts of "Patricia Roberts Cotton No.2" in each of the contrasts l. and n., 1 25 gram ball of "Patricia Roberts Angora" in contrast j. and a small amount of the same yarn in i. A pair each of size 2 and size 3 Aero knitting needles and a fine cable needle.

Colors

m. = pink, a. = shocking pink, b. = yellow, c. and g. = coral, d. = mauve, e. = orient blue, f. = aqua blue, h. = green, i. = dark gray, j. = mid gray, l. = white, n. = black.

Needle Sizes

Use size 3 needles for those referred to as size "A" and size 2 needles for those referred to as size "B" in the pattern.

SUMMER

Long Raj Cardigan

PHOTOGRAPH PAGE 63

Materials

25 25 gram balls of "Patricia Roberts Fine Cotton" in main color, 1 50 gram ball of "Patricia Roberts Cotton No.2" in each of the contrasts a., b., c., d., e., f., g. and h. and small amounts of "Patricia Roberts Cotton No.2" in contrasts l. and n.; plus 1 25 gram ball of "Patricia Roberts Angora" in contrast j. and a small amount in contrast i. A pair each of size 2 and size 3 Aero knitting needles, a fine cable needle and 9 buttons.

Colors

m. = white, a. = shocking pink, b. = yellow, c. = coral, d. = mauve, e. = orient blue, f. = aqua blue, g. = pink, h. = green, i. = dark gray, j. = mid gray, l. = white, n. = black.

Needle Sizes

Use size 3 needles for those referred to as size "A" and size 2 for those referred to as size "B".

Abbreviations

Cable 4, k.2, slip next 2 sts. onto cable needle at front of work, k.2, then k.2 from cable needle ■ **cable 10**, slip next 5 sts. onto a cable needle and leave at front of work, k.5, then k.5 from cable needle ■ **cr.2lt.**, cross 2 left thus, slip next 2 sts. onto cable needle at front of work, with m. k.2, with b. k.2 from cable needle ■ **cr.2rt.**, cross 2 right thus, slip next 2 sts. onto cable needle and leave at back of work, with b. k.2, then with m. k.2 from cable needle ■ **m.k.**, make knot thus, on **right side rows**, k.1, slip this st. back to left-hand needle and p.1, **on wrong side rows**, p.1, slip this st. back to left-hand needle and k.1 ■ **m.b.**, make bobble thus, with c. k. into back and front of st., turn, p.2, turn, k.2tog. ■ **2 from 2**, thus, working into front of sts., k.2tog. without dropping st. from left-hand needle, then working through back of same 2 sts., k.2tog. again.

Sweater Pattern

Short Raj Sweater

Tension

17 stitches and 21 rows to 2 in (5 cm) over the pattern using size "A" needles.

Measurements

Underarms: 40 in (100 cm). Side seam: 15 in (37.5 cm). Length: 24 in (60 cm). Sleeve seam: 16 in (40 cm).

Long Raj Sweater

Tension

16 stitches and 20 rows to 2 in (5 cm) over the pattern using size "A" needles.

Measurements
Underarms: 42½ in (106 cm). Side seam: 20 in (50 cm).
Length: 29½ in (74 cm). Sleeve seam: 17 in (42.5 cm).

Back
With size "B" needles and m. cast on 172 sts. and work
in pattern as follows:

1st to 4th rows: With m. all k.

5th row: K.10, ★ p.1, k.1, p.1, k.2, p.1, k.4, p.1, k.2,
p.1, k.1, p.1, k.2, p.1, k.4, p.1, k.2, p.1, k.1, p.1,
k.12; repeat from ★ ending last repeat k.10.

6th row: With m. k.2, p.4, k.2, ★ p.2, k.1, p.1, k.1,
p.2, k.1, p.4, k.1, p.2, k.1, p.1, k.1, p.2, k.1, p.4, k.1,
p.2, k.1, p.1, k.1, p.2, k.2, p.4, k.2; repeat from ★ to
end.

7th row: With m. k.2, cable 4, k.2, ★ p.3, k.1, p.4,
cable 4, p.4, k.1, p.4, cable 4, p.4, k.1, p.3, k.2, cable
4, k.2; repeat from ★ to end.

8th row: With m. k.2, p.4, k.5, ★ p.1, k.4, p.4, k.4,
p.1, k.4, p.4, k.4, p.1, k.5, p.4, k.5; repeat from ★
ending last repeat k.2.

Repeat the 5th to 8th rows 3 times more.

Change to size "A" needles and work in main pattern
as follows:

Use separate balls of contrast color for each section of
the pattern and separate balls of m. at each side of
color motifs.

1st to 8th rows: As 1st to 8th rows given before.

9th to 12th rows: As 5th to 8th rows.

13th to 16th rows: With m. all k.

For the Long Raj Sweater:

17th to 44th rows: Work in pattern from chart.

45th to 60th rows: With m. work as given for 1st to 16th
rows.

For the Short Raj Sweater:

The 17th to 60th rows are omitted.

For both Long and Short Raj Sweaters:

61st to 88th rows:

Work in pattern from chart.

89th to 104th rows: As given for 1st to 16th rows.

105th to 132nd rows: As given in chart.

133rd to 148th rows: As for 1st to 16th rows.

149th to 176th rows: As given in chart.

Now work the 1st to 6th pattern rows again.

To shape the armholes: Continuing in pattern, bind
off 8 sts. at the beginning of the next 2 rows.

On 156 sts. work the 9th to 16th rows.

Now work in yoke pattern as follows:

1st row: K.15, ★ p.1, k.1, p.1, k.38; repeat from ★
ending last repeat k.15.

2nd row: ★★ P.1, k.2, p.10, k.3, p.1, k.3, p.10, k.2,
p.1★, k.2, p.4, k.2; repeat from ★★ but ending last

repeat at ★.

3rd row: K.15, ★ p.1, k.1, p.1, k.17, cable 4, k.17;
repeat from ★ until 18 remain, p.1, k.1, p.1, k.15.

4th row: As 2nd row.

5th and 6th rows: As 1st and 2nd rows.

7th row: K.3, cable 10, k.2, p.1, k.1, p.1, k.2, cable 10,
★ k.5, cable 4, k.5, cable 10, k.2, p.1, k.1, p.1, k.2,
cable 10; repeat from ★ until 3 remain k.3.

8th row: As 2nd row.

9th to 20th rows: Repeat 1st to 4th rows, 3 times.

21st and 22nd rows: As 1st and 2nd rows.

23rd row: As 7th row.

24th row: As 2nd row.

25th to 28th rows: As 1st to 4th rows.

The last 28 rows form the cable pattern.★★★
Repeat them once more, then work the first 20 rows
again.

To slope the shoulders: Bind off 10 sts. at the
beginning of the next 10 rows.

Leave the remaining 56 sts. on a spare needle until
required.

Front

Work as given for back until ★★★ is reached. Repeat
the last 28 rows once more, then work the first row
again.

Now divide the sts. for the neck:

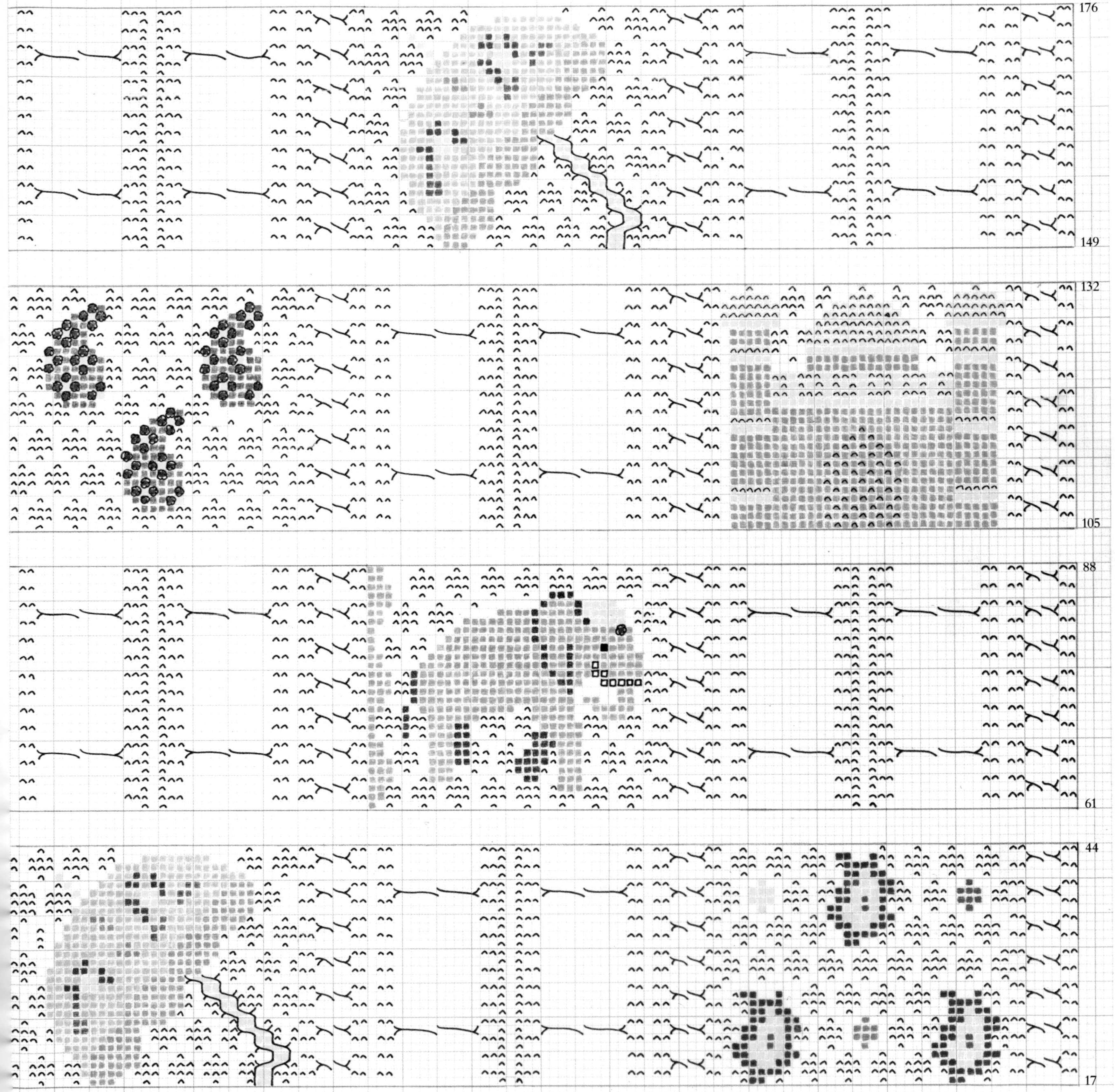
176
149
132
105
88
61
44
17

cr.2lt. with b. | a. | b. | c. | d. | e. | f. | g. | h. | j. | i. | l. | n.

cr.2rt. with b. | with a., m.k. | with c., m.b.

Next row: Pattern 64 sts. and leave these sts. on a spare needle until required for right front shoulder. Bind off 28 for the neck, pattern to end and continue on these 64 sts. for the left front shoulder.

Left front shoulder:

To shape the neck: Dec. 1 st. at the neck edge on the next 14 rows.

On 50 sts. work 4 rows.

To slope the shoulder: Bind off 10 sts. at the beginning of the next row and the 3 following alternate rows.

On 10 sts. work 1 row, then bind off.

Right front shoulder: With right side of work facing rejoin yarn to inner edge of sts. left on spare needle and pattern to end of row, then work as given for left front shoulder to end.

Collar or Neckband: First join right shoulder seam. With right side of work facing, rejoin m. to left shoulder and using size "B" needles pick up and k. 28 sts. from left front neck edge, 28 sts. from center front neck and 28 sts. from right front neck edge, then k. across the 56 sts. at back neck edge.

For the collar on Short Raj Sweater:

On 140 sts. work 73 rows in single rib, then bind off loosely in rib.

For the neckband on Long Raj Sweater:

On 140 sts. work 11 rows in single rib, then bind off loosely in rib.

S l e e v e s

Both alike: With size "B" needles and m. cast on 64 sts.

For the Long Raj Sweater:

K. 5 rows.

For both Long and Short Raj Sweaters:

Work 25 rows in single rib.

Increase row: Rib 5, ★ up 1, rib 6; repeat from ★ ending last repeat rib 5. [74 sts.]

Change to size "A" needles and work the first 10 rows of pattern given for yoke.

Continuing in yoke pattern as set and working the extra sts. in garter st. as they occur, inc. 1 st. at each end of the next row and then every 4th row 29 times.

On 134 sts. pattern 17 rows for the Short Raj Sweater or 13 rows for the Long Raj Sweater. Mark each end of the last row with colored threads.

Pattern 10 rows straight, then bind off loosely.

M a k i n g   U p

Do not press. Join left shoulder seam, continuing seam across collar or neckband. Set in sleeves, so that the row ends above marking threads are sewn to sts. bound off at underarms. Join sleeve and side seams.

C a r d i g a n   P a t t e r n

S h o r t   R a j   C a r d i g a n

T e n s i o n

16 stitches and 20 rows to 2 in (5 cm) over the pattern using size "A" needles.

M e a s u r e m e n t s

Underarms: 44½ in (111 cm). Side seam: 15¾ in (39 cm). Length: 25½ in (64 cm). Sleeve seam: 17 in (42.5 cm).

L o n g   R a j   C a r d i g a n

T e n s i o n

16 stitches and 20 rows to 2 in (5 cm) over the pattern using size "A" needles.

M e a s u r e m e n t s

Underarms: 44½ in (111 cm). Side seam: 20 in (50 cm). Length: 29½ in (74 cm). Sleeve seam: 17 in (42.5 cm).

B a c k

As given for back of Raj Sweater.

L e f t   F r o n t :

With size "B" needles and m., cast on 90 sts. and work as given for back until the 16th row of the main pattern has been worked.

For the Long Raj Cardigan:

17th row: With m. k.10, p.1, k.2, with a. k.2, with m. (k.3, p.1) 5 times, k.1, with a. k.2, with m. p.1, k.25, p.1, k.1, p.1, k.23.

18th row: With m. k.2, p.4, k.2, p.1, k.2, p.10, k.3, p.1, k.3, p.10, k.2, p.1, k.2, p.4, k.2, p.1, k.2, with a. p.4, with m. k.1, p.1, (k.3, p.1) 4 times, k.1, with a. p.4, with m. k.2, p.1, k.2, p.4, k.2.

The last 2 rows set the position of the pattern, given on the right-hand side of the chart. Now work the 19th to 176th pattern rows as set and given for back.

For the Short Raj Cardigan:

Omit the 17th to 60th rows and continue as follows:

61st row: With m. k.23, p.1, k.1, p.1, k.25, (p.1, k.3) 7 times, p.1, k.1, with e. k.1, with m. k.8.

62nd row: With m. k.2, p.4, k.2, with e. p.2, with m. k.2, (p.1, k.3) 7 times, p.1, k.2, p.4, k.2, p.1, k.2, p.10, k.3, p.1, k.3, p.10, k.2, p.1, k.2, p.4, k.2.

The last 2 rows set the position of the pattern, on the right-hand side of the chart. Work the 63rd to 176th rows as set and given for back.

For both Long and Short Raj Cardigans:
Work the first 6 pattern rows again.

To shape the armhole: Continuing in pattern as set, bind off 8 sts. at the beginning of the next row. On 82 sts. work the 8th to 16th rows.

Now work in yoke pattern as follows:
1st row: K.15, ★ p.1, k.1, p.1, k.38; repeat from ★ ending last repeat k.23.
2nd row: ★ K.2, p.4, k.2, p.1, k.2, p.10, k.3, p.1, k.3, p.10, k.2, p.1; repeat from ★ to end.
3rd row: K.15, ★ p.1, k.1, p.1, k.17, cable 4, k.17; repeat from ★ ending last repeat k.2.
4th row: As 2nd row.

The last 4 rows set the position of the yoke pattern given for back. Work the 5th to 28th rows.
Continuing in cable pattern, work 29 rows.

To shape the neck: Bind off 18 sts. at the beginning of the next row, then dec. 1 st. at the neck edge on the next 14 rows.
On 50 sts. work 4 rows.

To slope the shoulder: Bind off 10 sts. at the beginning of the next row and the 3 following alternate rows. On 10 sts. work 1 row, then bind off.

Buttonband: With size "B" needles and m. cast on 10 sts. and work 216 rows in single rib for the Short Raj Cardigan or 256 rows in single rib for the Long Raj Cardigan, then bind off.

Right Front

With size "B" needles and m., cast on 90 sts. and work as given for back until the 16th row of the main pattern has been worked.

For the Long Raj Cardigan:
17th row: With m. k.9, p.1, k.1, with b. k.2, with m. (p.1, k.3) 4 times, with e. k.3, with m. k.1, p.1, k.3, p.1, k.26, p.1, k.1, p.1, k.23.
The last row sets the position of the pattern, given on the left-hand side of the chart. Now work the 18th to 176th pattern rows as set and given for back.

For the Short Raj Cardigan:
Omit the 17th to 60th rows.
61st row: With m. k.23, p.1, k.1, p.1, k.23, with d. k.1, with m. k.4, p.1, k.3, p.1, k.2, with c. k.9, with m. p.1, (k.3, p.1) twice, k.2, with d. k.1, with m. k.8.
The last row sets the position of the pattern, given on the left-hand side of the chart. Now work the 62nd to 176th rows as set and given for back.

For both Long and Short Raj Cardigans:
Work the first 7 rows again.

To shape the armhole: Continuing in pattern as set, bind off 8 sts. at the beginning of the next row.
On 82 sts. work the 9th to 16th rows.

Now work in yoke pattern as follows:
1st row: K.23, ★ p.1, k.1, p.1, k.38; repeat from ★ ending last repeat k.15.
2nd row: ★ P.1, k.2, p.10, k.3, p.1, k.3, p.10, k.2, p.1, k.2, p.4, k.2; repeat from ★ to end.
3rd row: K.2, ★ cable 4, k.17, p.1, k.1, p.1, k.17; repeat from ★ ending last repeat k.15.
4th row: As 2nd row.

The last 4 rows set the position of the yoke pattern given for back. Work the 5th to 28th rows.
Continuing in cable pattern, work 30 rows.

To shape the neck: Work as given for left front neck shaping to end.

Buttonhole band: With size "B" needles and m. cast on 10 sts. and work 10 rows in single rib.
1st Buttonhole row: Rib 3, bind off 4, rib to end.
2nd Buttonhole row: Rib 3, turn, cast on 4, turn, rib to end.

For the Short Raj Cardigan:
Rib 32 rows. Repeat the last 34 rows 5 times more, then work the 2 buttonhole rows again. Rib 2 rows, then bind off.

For the Long Raj Cardigan:
Rib 28 rows. Repeat the last 30 rows 7 times, then work the 2 buttonhole rows again. Rib 4 rows, then bind off.

Sleeves

For the Short Raj Cardigan:
Work as given for sleeves of Short Raj Sweater.
For the Long Raj Cardigan:
Work as given for sleeves of Long Raj Sweater.

Making Up

Do not press. Join shoulder seams. Set in sleeves, so
that the row ends above the marking threads are sewn
to the sts. bound off at underarms. Join sleeve and side
seams. Neatly sew frontbands in place. Sew on
buttons.

Neckband

With right side of work facing, rejoin m. to right front
neck edge and using size "B" needles pick up and k. 44
sts. from top of buttonhole band and right front neck
edge, k. across the 56 sts. at back neck edge, then pick
up and k. 44 sts. from left front neck edge and
buttonband. On 144 sts. work 4 rows in single rib.
Next row: Rib 2, sl.1, k.2tog., p.s.s.o., rib until 5
remain, sl.1, k.2tog., p.s.s.o., rib 2.
Next row: Rib to end.
Repeat the last 2 rows twice more, then work the first
of these rows again.
Bind off the remaining 128 sts. loosely in rib.

t e a r o s e

Delicate rose motifs are scattered all over this T-shirt. Knitted in a combination of lambswool and angora for winter, its spring and summer variations use cool cotton.

W I N T E R

T e a R o s e T - S h i r t

PHOTOGRAPH THIS PAGE

Materials
16 (17) 25 gram balls of "Patricia Roberts Lambswool No.1" in main color, plus 2 balls of "Patricia Roberts Angora" in each of the contrasts a. and b. and 1 ball of the same yarn in each of the contrasts c., d., e. and f. A pair each of size 1 and size 3 Aero knitting needles.

Colors
m. = shocking pink Lambswool, a. = shocking pink Angora, b. = red, c. = purple, d. = grape, e. = orange, f. = yellow.

Needle Sizes
Use size 3 needles for those referred to as size "A" and size 1 needles for those referred to as size "B" in the pattern.

S P R I N G

T e a R o s e T - S h i r t

PHOTOGRAPH PAGE 29

Materials
11 (12) 25 gram balls of "Patricia Roberts Extra Fine Cotton" in main color and 2 balls of "Patricia Roberts Fine Cotton" in contrast a., plus 2 50 gram balls of "Patricia Roberts Cotton No.2" in contrast b. and 1 ball of each of the contrasts c., d., e. and f. A pair each of size 1 and size 2 Aero knitting needles.

Colors
m. = mustard, a. = blue Fine Cotton, b. = blue Cotton No.2, c. = khaki, d. = coral, e. = mauve, f. = mustard. Note that m. and f. are in the same color on this version.

WINTER

Tea Rose T-Shirt
RIGHT

SPRING

Tea Rose T-Shirt
PAGE 29

SUMMER

Tea Rose T-Shirt
PAGE 62

Needle Sizes

Use size 2 needles for those referred to as size "A" and size 1 needles for those referred to as size "B" in the pattern.

SUMMER

Tea Rose T-Shirt

PHOTOGRAPH PAGE 62

Materials

11 (12) 25 gram balls of "Patricia Roberts Extra Fine Cotton" in main color and 2 balls of "Patricia Roberts Fine Cotton" in contrast a., plus 2 50 gram balls of "Patricia Roberts Cotton No.2" in contrast b. and 1 ball in each of the contrasts c., d., e. and f. A pair each of size 1 and size 2 Aero knitting needles.

Colors

m. = white, a. = red, b. = shocking pink, c. = olive, d. = mauve, e. = coral, f. = mustard.

Needle Sizes

Use size 2 needles for those referred to as size "A" and size 1 needles for those referred to as size "B" in the pattern.

Abbreviations

m.k., make knot thus, on wrong side rows, with d. p.1, sl. this st. to left-hand needle and k.1.

Tension

16 stitches and 20 rows to 2 in (5 cm) over the stockinette stitch using size "A" needles.

T-Shirt Pattern

Measurements

Underarms: (Small) 44 in (110 cm). (Large) 49½ in (124 cm). Side seam: 17 in (42.5 cm). Length: 26½ in (66 cm). Sleeve seam: 3½ in (8.5 cm).

Back

With size "B" needles and m. cast on 178 (200) sts. and work in moss st. as follows:
1st row: ★ K.1, p.1; repeat from ★ to end.
2nd row: ★ P.1, k.1; repeat from ★ to end.
Repeat these 2 rows 6 times more.
Change to size "A" needles and work in pattern as

follows. The pattern is worked in s.s., except where indicated, so only the color details are given. Use separate small balls of color for each motif, so that colors not in use are not taken across the back of the work.
1st to 7th rows: All m.
8th row: With wrong side of work facing, 34 (12) m., ★ 1 c., 43 m.; repeat from ★ ending last repeat 11 m.
9th row: 10 m., ★ 3 c., 41 m.; repeat from ★ ending last repeat 33 (11) m.
10th row: 33 (11) m., ★ 3 c., 41 m.; repeat from ★ ending last repeat 10 m.
11th to 39th rows: Work in pattern from chart as set.
40th row: 8 (30) m., ★ 1 c., 43 m.; repeat from ★ ending last repeat 37 m.
41st row: 36 m., ★ 3 c., 41 m.; repeat from ★ ending last repeat 7 (29) m.
42nd to 68th rows: Work in pattern from chart as set.
The last 68 rows form the pattern; repeat them once more then work the first 20 rows again. Mark each end of the last row with colored threads to denote armholes.
To shape the armholes: Maintaining the continuity of the pattern, dec. 1 st. at each end of the next 22 rows. ★★ On 134 (156) sts. pattern 64 rows.
To slope the shoulders: Bind off 9 (11) sts. at the beginning of the next 8 rows. [62 (68) sts.]
Bind off the remaining 62 (68) sts.

Front

Work as given for the back until ★★ is reached. On 134 (156) sts. pattern 33 rows.
Now divide the sts. for the neck:
Next row: Pattern 56 (64) sts. and leave these sts. on a spare needle until required for right front shoulder, bind off 22 (28) sts., pattern to end and continue on these 56 (64) sts. for the left front shoulder.
Left front shoulder: To shape the neck: Dec. 1 st. at the neck edge on each of the next 11 rows and the 9 following alternate rows.
On 36 (44) sts. work 1 row.
To slope the shoulder: Bind off 9 (11) sts. at the beginning of the next row and the 2 following alternate rows. On 9 (11) sts. work 1 row, then bind off.
Right front shoulder: With right side of work facing, rejoin yarn to inner edge of sts. left on spare needle and work to end of row, then work as given for left front shoulder to end.
Neckband: With right side of work facing, rejoin m. to left front shoulder and using size "B" needles, pick up and k. 34 sts. from left neck edge, 20 (24) sts. from center front neck edge, 34 sts. from right front neck

edge and 54 (60) sts. from back neck edge.
On 142 (152) sts. work 9 rows in moss st. as given for back, then bind off loosely.

Sleeves

Both alike: With size "B" needles and m. cast on 134 sts. and work 10 rows in moss st. as for back. Change to size "B" needles and work 24 rows in rose pattern as given for small size on back. Mark each end of the last row with colored threads to denote the sleeve top.

To shape the sleeve top: Maintaining the continuity of the pattern as set, dec. 1 st. at each end of the next 40 rows. [54 sts.]
Bind off 3 sts. at the beginning of the next 4 rows and 8 sts. on the 4 following rows. Bind off the remaining 10 sts.

Making Up

Join shoulder seams. Set in sleeves, matching marking threads on sleeves to those on back and front. Join sleeve and side seams.

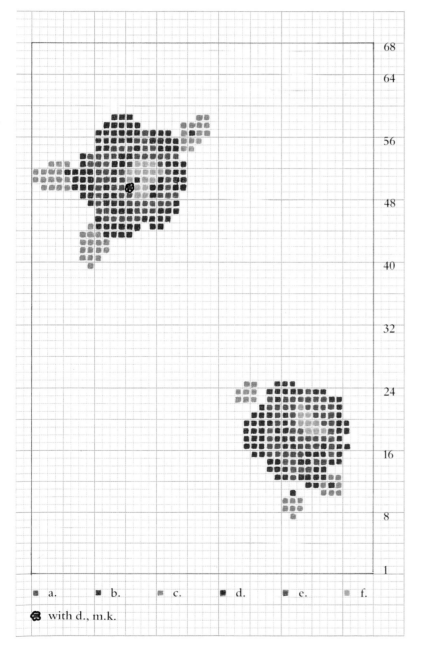

winter variations

Kashmir Vest Paisley Sweater

LEFT
Cream cashmere creates a supremely elegant version of the Kashmir Vest. The man wears a cream wool variation on the Paisley design.
PATTERNS PAGE 42 AND PAGE 50

Alpine Sweater

RIGHT
Motifs of a tree, a skier and a house, worked in the same color as the main pattern, make this roll-neck sweater ideal for winter sports or *après ski*.
PATTERN PAGE 112

Long Twist Sweater Spaghetti Sweater

OVERLEAF
The woman wears a cream wool version of the Twist design; the man's comfortable sweater is the Spaghetti design.
PATTERNS PAGE 132 AND PAGE 138

Sources

For mail order and to obtain a current list of suppliers of Patricia Roberts' yarns and knitting kits, please contact:

STACEY CHARLES COLLECTION
119 Green Street
Brooklyn, NY 11222
Tel: 718-389-0411
Fax: 718-389-0416

Yarns and made-up garments are also available from:

TANGLEWOOL
57 Church Street
Lenox, MA 01240
Tel: 413-637-0900

PATRICIA ROBERTS
60 Kinnerton Street
Knightsbridge
London SW1X 6ES
England
Tel: 071-235-4742
Fax: 071-235-6517

a c k n o w l e d g m e n t s

Photography by Vittoria Amati
Pages: 1, 12, 13, 14, 15, 16, 18, 19, 30, 31, 33, 34, 35, 84, 86, 87, 90, 110

Models: Benedetta; Amy; John Fontein; Yoshihiko Hibino

Hair: Vicky at Smile

Photography by Sam Brown
Pages: 9 below, 10 center, 13, 20, 21, 22, 24, 25, 26, 27, 32, 36, 37, 39, 41, 42, 43, 45, 46, 47, 85, 89, 91, 92, 93, 96, 97, 98, 99, 100, 101, 104, 107, 108, 111, 112, 113, 114, 116, 117, 118, 119

Models: Samantha Goldberg; Lisa Cummins

Hair and make-up: Kevin Dolman

Photography by Sheila Rock
Pages: 3, 5 above left, 6, 7, 8 above, 9 above and center, 10 above and below, 11 above and center, 28, 29, 48, 49, 50, 51, 52, 54, 56, 57, 58, 59, 60, 61, 62, 63, 64, 65, 67, 69, 70, 71, 73, 74, 75, 76, 79, 80, 81, 82, 83

Models: Tess; Karen; Bronwyn; Nando del Castillo

Hair and make-up: Alfredo Apolinaris; Marybeth Miermeister

Pages: 2, 5, 8 center and below, 11 below, 120, 121, 122, 123, 124, 128, 129, 130, 131, 132, 133, 135, 136, 137, 138, 139, 140, 141, 142, 143, 145, 146, 148, 150, 151, 152, 153, 155, 156, 157, 158

Models: Lisa B; Marcel; Cal

Hair and make-up: Kraige Fairbairn

Stylist: Caroline Baker
Assistant (for Sam Brown photography): Amanda Bellan

The publishers would like to thank the following for lending clothes for photography:

Karen Boyd; Katherine Hamnett; Harrods; Betty Jackson; Oilily; Rifat Ozbek; Helen Storey; Chrissy Walsh; Whistles

With thanks to: Bibendum Restaurant, Fulham Road, London SW3 and Wormwood Scrubs Pony Centre, East Acton Lane, London W3 for their help with locations; M. Conti's dog.